Contents

Author's Note

Without the kindness, interest and support of those involved in the companies and other authors who have allowed me to use research material I would not have been able to complete this book. Without people being prepared to give me their time and knowledge of times past then the book would have been very bland – it is the anecdotes about the founders and those who followed that bring the stories to life.

The list of people I thank privately is indeed extensive, but I would publicly like to thank the following who gave me photographs and memorabilia:

John Beale (pp 48, 49), Ian Dewhirst (p 37, top), Stuart Eaden-Allen (pp 46, 47), HKP Lines (p 62, bottom), Wendy Priest (p 62, top), Westminster Archives (pp 78–80, 87–89).

Additionally I would very much like to thank Alison Adburgham, Harold Baker, T W Baker-Jones, David Binns, Jenny and Trevor Bryan, Jeremy J Burton, Andrew Coker, Sean Callery, Rob Dyer, Nat Garrett, Susanna Geoghegan, Dorothy Greaves, Tom and Peggy Hewitt, Dr Fred Kidd, Marylebone Cricket Club, Ken Morrison, Manchester University Press, Don Mosey, Monty Moss, Fred Redding, Anne Sebba, Angela Shipston, Steven Simpson, Malcolm Speed, Debbie Taylor, and the staff of Michael O'Mara Books Limited, particularly Lesley O'Mara and Annabel Reid for all their support and help.

If anyone feels I have failed to give them credit I do apologize, it has not been done intentionally. It is often difficult to get everything in order.

Without my wife's help the task would not only be less enjoyable, but Judith also keeps me going when there are days when you feel like giving up! Thank you for making book number three possible.

This book is dedicated to my mother, Dorothy Lilian Baren, in this her ninetieth year. For all her love and kindness to me and all the family, our sincere thanks.

Bibliography

ADBURGHAM, ALISON, *Liberty's A Biography of a Shop* (Unwin Hyman)

CALLERY, SEAN, *Harrods – The Story of Society's Favourite Store* (Ebury Press)

DOBSON, O R, *A Hundred Years of the Halifax* (Batsford)

MOSEY, DON and RAMSDEN, HARRY, *Harry Ramsden* (Dalesman)

POWELL, DAVID, *Counter Revolution – The Tesco Story* (Grafton Books)

RODDICK, ANITA, *Body & Soul* (The Body Shop)

SEBBA, ANNE, *Laura Ashley – A Life by Design* (Wiedenfeld & Nicholson)

SIEFF, MARCUS, *Don't Ask the Price* (Wiedenfeld & Nicholson)

SIGSWORTH, ERIC, *Montague Burton – Tailor of Taste* (Manchester University Press)

Introduction

'Gone to the shops' – how often we leave, or find, notes like that; it has been said we are a nation of shopkeepers, and shoppers!

Anita Roddick has not only a passion for The Body Shop, but also for a variety of causes, both in distant small countries and in England; it was Thomas Cook's passion for the temperance movement which was to lead him into the role of being the first travel agent. William Fortnum's royal connections helped him establish a high-class grocer's shop, whilst Jesse Boot's concern for the poor was the foundation of his 'prescription' service.

In our high streets, and in our capital city, we find many familiar names. Some businesses have been trading for over 200 years whilst others first welcomed their customers less than twenty-five years ago. Famous stores, such as Harrods and Selfridges, cater for our specialist wants, whilst the likes of Sainsbury's and Tesco satisfy our families' needs. Each is an important part of our lives. Our financial institutions often come from very diverse origins, and the presence of Lloyds, Abbey National and the Yorkshire Bank illustrate some of these factors.

A number of the stories have never been written down and very many of the illustrations have not previously been published. All are part of our rich heritage, our social history. The personal stories, the anecdotes and private papers tell us so much of those who formed the townscape we know today.

Austin Reed knew what it was to be a shopkeeper, for in his last days he wrote: 'The "goodwill" of a business is its most valuable asset. It cannot be purchased with money. It can only be built into the fabric of the business by the application of sound principles and by patient service . . . Let no word or deed of yours detract from the reputation for fair and honest dealing, and willing and courteous service which our business possesses and which is your inheritance.'

Maurice Baren 1996

The building society movement dates from the formation of Building Clubs in 1775 in Birmingham. Regular subscriptions were collected from members until enough money had been raised to build houses for everyone. Once this was achieved, the society wound up. Permanent building societies were not established until 1845, servicing both investors and borrowers, the investors and borrowers becoming separate groups, using the society for different purposes.

The National Building Society was formed in 1849 in the names of four trustees. Within its first few months thousands of people were clamouring to invest their money, not necessarily wanting to build homes, but rather hoping to gain a 'freehold estate', for from medieval times anyone owning freehold land valued at forty shillings a year was entitled to vote. The society was being used for political reform.

Initially the society was registered as the National Permanent Mutual Benefit Building Society, later being known as the Freehold Land Society. Over £20,000 was subscribed during the first year, rising to a staggering £1.5 million after ten years, as estates were bought, such as New Malden, Kingston, Uxbridge, Enfield and Godalming. During 1800–51 the population doubled to sixteen million, half being resident in urban areas. Average incomes similarly doubled and, with the growth of the railways, communication between towns greatly improved. It was the railways which provided the link between the new housing developments and the city where people worked.

The Abbey Road Building Society saw its birth in a Baptist chapel in Kilburn, London. A young but powerful preacher,Yorkshireman William Stott, was persuaded to take on a Baptist mission at the age of eighteen. One of his first tasks was to build a chapel under which was a large schoolroom providing a meeting place for community projects, including the Abbey Road Benefit Society. On 8 March 1874 twelve people met to discuss Frank Yerbury's idea of forming a building society. Revd William Stott was invited to become its first president. The first rule the society laid down was that subscriptions had to be one shilling per week on each share, to be paid every Wednesday evening between 8.30 and 9.30pm at the society's office, i.e. the schoolroom.

The Building Societies Act 1874, the 'Magna Carta', tightened up the ways in which societies had to act. Previously many people rented their homes, but now there was a growing desire for home ownership, particularly among tradesmen and shopkeepers. In many cases these people bought rows of terrace houses, the rents from these

FACING PAGE: *Abbey Road Building Society badge*
RIGHT: *Early advertisement*

providing an income for them in their retirement, or perhaps providing homes for unmarried or orphaned members of their families. The Act declared that societies had to prepare annual statements of receipts and expenditure, and also that no society could own land or buildings except for offices.

Officially the society became known as The Abbey Road and St John's Wood Mutual Benefit Building Society, which later changed to The Abbey Road and St John's Wood Permanent Building Society. A seal of a lighthouse within a circle was designed and the motto 'Unity, Equity and Stability' taken up. Their first real office was at 16 Finchley Road, London.

During the 1880s, as the middle-class population grew and the housing boom continued, developers found that landowners, such as Eton College, were very willing to let their land be built on in return for the high returns they received. At the peak in 1903, 150,000 properties were built, although this declined to only 48,000 in 1914. At that time mortgages were normally for no more than two-thirds of the value of the property, with repayments spread over eight to fourteen years.

Both societies were innovative, the National being among the first to introduce mortgage protection insurance plans, whereby both the society and the borrower were protected.

In 1922 Harold Bellman, a human dynamo, having worked for Lloyd George and Winston Churchill and been awarded the MBE at the age of thirty-four, was appointed secretary of the Abbey Road. Other directors included a retired coachman, an ironmonger, a draper and a police-court-journalist. Within a short period of time the society became second only to the Halifax Permanent and Equitable.

Between 1924 and 1930 no less than 1.3 million homes were built, 880,000 of these by private housebuilders. Such housebuilding was supported by the new Metropolitan Railway network which opened the whole of the area to the north west of London for suburban development. Mortgages were now extended to ninety per cent of the value of the property with repayment periods being extended to twenty years, and in some cases twenty-five.

Harold Bellman made arrangements with the Brotherhood of Free Churches to collect savings and make advances to their members. In 1925 the society took a stand at the *Daily Mail* Ideal Home Exhibition and branches opened in Watford, Reading, Southend and Blackpool.

Both societies had head offices in Moorgate, but in 1932 the Abbey Road opened a magnificent new building, complete with a huge campanile, with its own peal of bells, some 150 feet high. Its original lighthouse emblem was carved over the imposing main entrance, while in its lower ground floor were a series of strong rooms holding securities worth more than £60 million.

The early 1930s brought low interest rates and cheap mortgages but still the costs made owning homes difficult for working-class people. One scheme developed to help in such circumstances was a 'pool', which covered a number of houses, often a whole estate. Mortgages could now be raised to ninety-five per cent with down payments of as little as £25, including legal fee. Monthly repayments could be as low as £1.

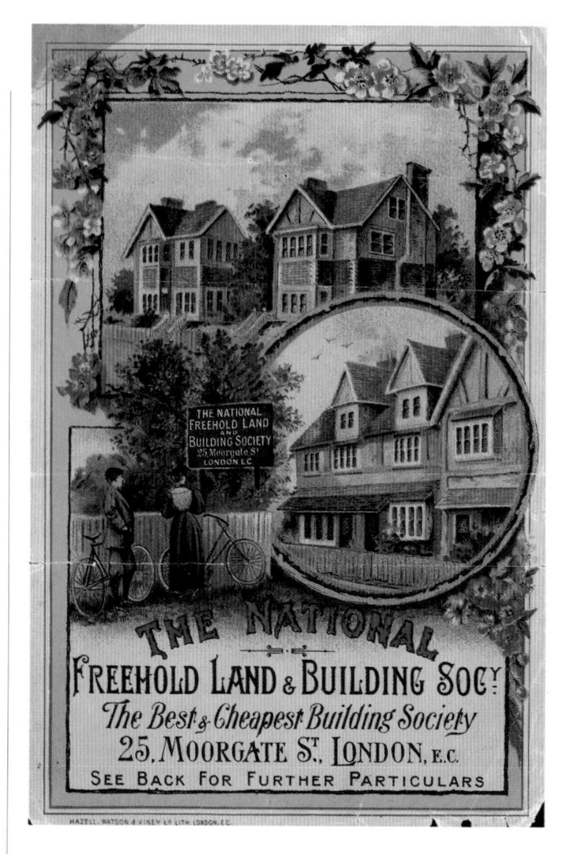

On New Year's Day 1944 the two societies merged and Harold Bellman became their first chairman. Post-war building required economies of scale. After the war, however, the Labour Government made building societies the subject of an ideological attack. 'Council-house' building was to be financed by the state. When the Conservatives returned to power in 1951 they pledged to build a massive 300, 000 houses a year. By the end of 1962 the society's assets had risen from £80 million at the time of the merger to £500 million.

In 1959 Stanley Morton, the society's general manager, had said that he did not believe that any single society could justify having its own computer, but in 1963, as the society became modernized, they installed a Honeywell computer. Today they have thousands, giving a network of information between branches and head office. On the

FACING PAGE TOP, AND THIS PAGE: *Early advertising*
FACING PAGE, BOTTOM: *'Our building stands well' motto and coat of arms*

sudden death of Stanley Morton in 1975, the last of the powerful, almost dictatorial leaders of the society, Lord Hill of Luton, who had been known to millions as the 'radio doctor', but now a Conservative Minister, was appointed his successor.

The society gradually became modernized. By 1979 there were more than 500 branches nationwide. House prices rose that same year by a phenomenal 27.5%.

During the 1980s, Sir Campbell Adamson became chairman and Clive Thornton became the new chief general manager. The Abbey National sign was registered in Europe and a representative office opened in Brussels, the first British building society to do so. 'Housing action' programmes were inaugurated where the society worked very closely with local authorities on housing renewal. By 1982 the society had 664 branches, in addition to 2463 agencies, and by 1984 all of these were on-line to the central computer.

In 1984 the Building Societies Association issued proposals that while Building Societies should retain their primary function as mortgage providers they should be allowed a wider range of functions such as estate agencies, conveyancing and certain retail banking facilities. It also proposed that societies should be able to convert to companies, from their mutual status. These proposals became law in the Building Societies Act 1986.

In 1988 the board agreed to the society becoming a public limited company. Five million members were entitled to vote on the proposal, and this became the largest private poll ever conducted. Its shares were marketed on 12 July, being subscribed 2.7 times, and the company story of Abbey National PLC had begun.

Today the Abbey National Treasury Services raises money on the international money markets. To enable them to enter more fully into the sale of insurance projects, they acquired the Scottish Mutual Assurance in 1991, and now offer their product through independent financial advisers. In 1993 Abbey National Life was set up to sell life insurance and pension products.

The name Aquascutum comes from the Latin, *aqua* meaning 'water', and *scutum* meaning 'shield'. Aquascutum's unique woollen fabric was showerproof, while being air-permeable and supple.

The origin of Aquascutum is clearly connected with two companies which occupied premises at 46 & 48 Regent Street around the period of the Great Exhibition of 1851. John Emary & Co took over the business and premises from a Daniel Bax, tailor and draper. In a business directory for 1850 Daniel Bax & Co had a gutta-percha warehouse at 89 Holborn Hill (gutta-percha being a means of waterproofing material but which caused the wearer to sweat), while an Edward Bax had a mackintosh and parama (*sic*) warehouse, and was also an umbrella and India-rubber golosh maker. Fennell & Emary also had a gutta-percha warehouse. Alison Adburgham, in *Shops and Shopping*, states that Bax & Co sold the invention and business premises to Emary & Co prior to April 1852. She also states that the original chemical formula, together with both Aquascutum's records and those of the Patent Office, were destroyed during German enemy action.

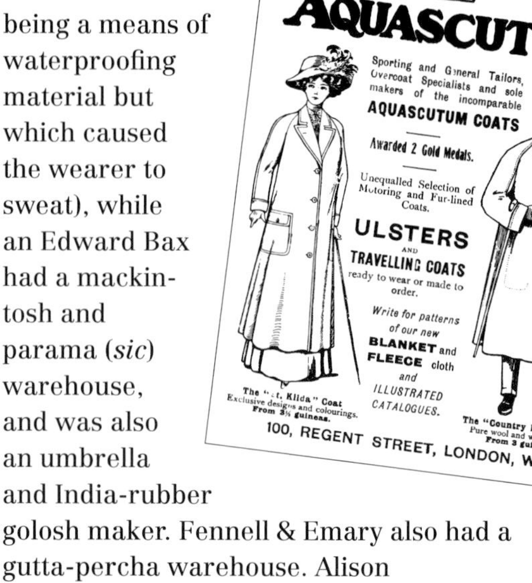

Aquascutum coats soon became fashionable among gentlemen. When officers went to war with the Russians in the Crimea in 1855 they took with them their Aquascutum overcoats as protection from the bone-chilling winters. Indeed, there is a story told of a Captain Goodlake and his sergeant who became involved in a skirmish with the Russians and were surrounded by them. To their surprise the Russians paid them no attention, their coats being indistinguishable from the enemy's.

Edward, Prince of Wales, later King Edward VII, being a leader of fashion, was to play an important part in promoting garments of Aquascutum cloth as fashion items for the English aristocracy. The company received it first Royal Warrant from the prince in 1897.

FACING PAGE, TOP: *Ladies' and gentlemen's coats*
FACING PAGE, BOTTOM: *John Emary*
RIGHT: *100 Regent Street, London*

For the army officers of the First World War, Aquascutum produced the trench coat, a classic style, which also played its part in keeping the forces warm and dry during the Second World War, especially those serving in places such as Iceland and Norway. They also made coats for sailors on winter convoys and jackets for airmen on night-long bombing raids. The trench coat is still worn today by both men and women.

By 1901 Aquascutum had moved to 100 Regent Street, which is still occupied by Aquascutum today. The prestigious corner site, occupied by the jewellers Shepheard & Co for about forty years, was finally acquired by Aquascutum in 1924, the total premises becoming known as 100 Regent Street. Aquascutum Ltd was incorporated on 14 November 1901, and a charter recording this is displayed in the store.

In 1923 the Crown Commissioners let it be known that all the shopkeepers, who were only leaseholders, either had to rebuild to a set design or get out! Aquascutum's fine new premises were reopened in 1927, but even then the Crown Commissioners refused to renew the lease. The building stuck out into Regent Street by quarter of an inch too much! Aquascutum offered to have the offending section removed with a hammer and chisel, but in due course the matter was dropped.

In 1948 Aquascutum opened a showroom in New York's Empire State Building – later to move to Fifth Avenue; shops have opened around the world in Montreal, Toronto, Ottawa and Chicago, Singapore, Hong Kong, Dublin and Paris. Two-thirds of their business is in export trade and for their outstanding trade they have received five Queen's Awards for export achievement. The company holds a Royal Warrant granted by Queen Elizabeth The Queen Mother and in 1982 was awarded the prestigious Grant of Arms.

Aquascutum has a great history but is also working hard to ensure it has an equally great future. During the last half-century special orders have been fulfilled which have helped Sir Edmund Hilary and Sherpa Tensing Norkey to conquer Everest and similarly allowed Sir Vivian Fuchs to complete his trek to the South Pole. Later developments have been Aqua 5, a process which has eliminated the need for garments to be re-proofed after dry-cleaning. Today its range of clothing covers all events of life, both for men and women, from the sporting to the most important social occasion. Its latest styles are also developed in such a way that they can be accompanied by a full range of coordinated accessories.

Asprey

The Asprey family was one of many Protestant families to leave France and settle in England during the eighteenth century. Two families of Aspreys came across the Channel, one settling in Mitcham, the other in Olney, between Bedford and Northampton.

The family who settled in Mitcham were originally calico printers. At the beginning of the nineteenth century, however, the character of Mitcham was changing and new industries included the Mizen's Glass House, the Surrey Iron Railway, and later in the century Pain's Fireworks. It is therefore not surprising that Charles Asprey and his son, also called Charles, chose to work in these fields. They went into business together and in 1839 they are described as Asprey & Son, Ironmonger & Smith.

By 1841 Charles Asprey I must have felt confident that he was doing quite well financially for he entered into a partnership with a high-class stationer, Francis Kennedy, at 49 New Bond Street in London. Five years later Charles Asprey II joined him, the year after his son, Charles Asprey III, was born. The next year, in 1847, they moved to 166 New Bond Street.

Old Bond Street was built in 1686 with New Bond Street being built in two phases, the first soon after 1700, the second to Oxford Street about 1721. The street's name is taken from Sir Thomas Bond, who was its first developer. Soon Bond Street was a bustling place of trade and commerce. Along its length were to be found galleries and bookshops, provision merchants, as well as homes for the rich and famous – it was the 'right' address to have. Other shops served the everyday needs, the milliners, drapers, cutlers, butchers, chemists and jewellers. At No 50 was Chappell, 'Music Seller to Her Majesty', the only firm still there today.

In 1859 Aspreys took over Edwards of King Street in Holborn who had won a gold medal for a gentleman's dressing case at the Great Exhibition of 1851. Aspreys later took over another prestigious dressing case maker, W Leuchars, who in turn owned Dee's, a wholesale jewellers.

In 1861 they acquired the rooms of the Alfred Club at 22 Albemarle Street, which backs onto Bond Street, giving a shop which stretched between two streets. With the development of rail travel there was a move towards the making of leather travelling cases for the gentry, some with intricate designs inlaid with tortoise-shell costing as much as £400. Aspreys now acquired the lease of 15a Grafton Street, running along the end of Bond Street and Albermarle Street, offering additional frontage. Gradually Aspreys acquired more and more of the neighbouring premises.

Many ruling heads of Europe, in England for the funeral of King Edward VII, shopped at Aspreys. When George V came to the throne, George Asprey would personally wait upon Queen Mary. As elsewhere, trade during the First World War suffered, but a military department supplying camp equipment was formed and this had a caravan-marquee which was sent to the Salisbury Plain Camp to make sales.

Aspreys became a limited company in 1909. Americans and Indian maharajahs were among the big spenders. One order came from the Maharaja of Patiala for five teak trunks, each to be fitted with silver washing and bathing utensils – one for each of his wives. Haile Selassie was also among many overseas clients.

In 1974 Aspreys opened in Geneva. In 1975 the firm was awarded the Queen's Award for Industry for outstanding export achievement. Aspreys still specializes in luxury goods, their major market being the Arab world. The work is carried out in their factory where you might also see the perfect scale of Concorde created in silver; a model, in gold, of the first floating oil derrick, or jewelled kingfishers, hummingbird clocks and golden elephants.

In 1988 Apreys went public and has since bought Mappin & Webb and Watches of Switzerland. In 1995 the company was taken over by Prince Jefri Bolkiah of Brunei, but John Asprey continues to manage and direct the company.

FACING PAGE, TOP: *Charles Asprey I*
FACING PAGE, BOTTOM: *Aspreys, Bond Street, London*
ABOVE: *Asprey Princess Diamond Egg, containing 220.21 cts, which took three years to complete*

AUSTIN REED

In 1853 Thomas Reed, a Cornishman, came to Reading and opened a hat shop. His son, William, expanded the company to include a small hosiery outlet and became sole London agent for the 'Registered Perfect Fitting Shirt', an early attempt to develop an off-the-peg shirt. In 1876 the business had become Thomas Reed & Son, hatters and hosiers and in 1881 they had moved into double-fronted premises, 100 Broad Street.

William's son, Austin Leonard, followed in the family tradition, first gaining invaluable experience and inspiration from America. As a junior at Wanamaker's in Philadelphia, Austin was impressed by the spectacular window displays, bulk purchasing and the retail pricing system.

In 1896 Austin returned to England and began working for his father in the shop. The relationship was rather strained, however, Austin being rather arrogant. The ambitious young man persuaded his father to buy William Stambrook & Son, a shirtmakers and hosiers in Fenchurch Street, in

London. Austin was now twenty-six years old and on 7 July 1900 opened for business at 167 Fenchurch Street. It was the start of Austin Reed.

He had done his market research during those early years in London and knew what his customers wanted and how to attract them. He stocked the newest styles in hats and collars and knew the importance of design and cut. He made a special point of getting to know his clients, the young city clerks and their superiors.

Two of the young men from the Reading shops also moved in, literally, for they slept under the counters during the week and returned to their homes at the weekends. The first week, Austin opened on the Saturday, travelled home by train and on Sunday joined his family at Reading Congregational Church, giving thanks for what he had received and praying for God's blessing in the future. That Sunday night he caught the last train to London, ready to open on the Monday morning. By the end of the first year his turnover had reached nearly £4000, which was doubled in the second year.

As soon as Austin was given control of the whole company in 1905, he sold the Reading shops and bought 13 Fenchurch Street. The business began trading as Austin Reed. It was a considerable risk for he had to treble salaries and overheads and it needed a costly refurbishment. Building on his American experience, Austin called his window displays 'pictures' and in them he used attractive show cards and price tickets which were hand-written or printed by his own staff. He used direct mail shots,

the whole mailing list of some 15,000 names in 1909 receiving from four to six shots, the names of course being held on a card system.

In 1910 a third shop was opened in Cheapside and in that same year he moved his offices to 19 Nicholl Square, a four-storey building which also served as a warehouse. Also in 1910, Austin Reed became a private company, Austin giving himself a ten-year contract as managing director. He was regarded as a good, though demanding, employer, engendering an immense sense of loyalty. He was later to introduce a staff pension scheme, one of the first in Britain. Soon shops opened in London's Oxford Street and Regent Street, followed by stores in Birmingham and Manchester.

FACING PAGE, TOP: *Reed & Son poster*
FACING PAGE, BOTTOM: *13 Fenchurch Street, London*
ABOVE: *Advertisement from the 1930s*

LEFT: *Winton Churchill's siren suit*
FACING PAGE: *Austin Reed symbol, 1903*

Austin Reed went into liquidation on 31 May 1920 so that subscription lists could be opened for a new public company of the same name. Austin was now forty-six years old and in a hurry to expand. For two years, profits declined, failing to meet the promise of the prospectus, but new branches were opening all over England.

As the City acknowledged Reed's recovery, so the undersubscribed shares were soon taken up. Again, Austin went to the United States for inspiration, introducing his 'New Tailoring', his euphemism for 'ready-to-wear' clothing, combining a wide choice of the best cloth with the latest styles in over 100 fittings. The changing room was brought in.

The Regent Street department store became the Austin Reed flagship, the height of excellence and distinction, complete with art-deco balconies in the shape of wing collars and a lift shaft by the sculptor Joseph Emberton.

1930 heralded the beginning of a world-wide recession and it was also the year Austin's son, Douglas Austine Reed, became a director. He had already been extremely successful in servicing agents in Europe and Scandinavia and gaining many influential customers including Robert Menzies, Pandit Nehru and Jomo Kenyatta. Cunard invited Austin Reed to take up a franchise to operate a branch on the transatlantic liner *Aquitania*; later concessions were taken on both the *Queen Mary* and *Queen Elizabeth*.

As a member of the Moral Re-Armament Movement, which advocated a total regard to honesty, purity, unselfishness and love, according to the teachings of Jesus, the declaration of war in 1939 caused Austin great sorrow. At one meeting he described how he had overhauled his entire price structure in his shops because he was charging too much. He also became profoundly aware of social disparities and had his own strong views on how the British economy should be run.

As a result of damage and low stock during the war, it was decided to start stocking women's clothes and other 'special' war-time orders, including outfits for special agents and members of the resistance groups, but their most famous order was the one-piece siren suit for Winston Churchill. It was so successful that he ordered a formal one in velvet!

In 1948, at the age of seventy-five, Austin Reed handed over the chairmanship to Herbert Kidson. In 1950 the company celebrated its Golden Jubilee, and in the in-house magazine, *The Tie*, Austin Reed wrote: 'The "goodwill" of a business is its most valuable asset. It cannot be purchased with money. It can only be built into the fabric of the business by the application of sound principles and by patient service . . . Let no word or deed of yours detract from the reputation for fair and honest dealing, and willing and courteous service which our business possesses and which is your inheritance.'

In the mid-1950s a third generation of the Reed family started to bring to the company new ideas and enthusiasm, Barry Reed becoming company chairman in 1973. Over the next twenty years Austin Reed continued to provide fashionable clothes for men and women. Gradually the number of branches grew as they took over established shops in provincial centres. Trading links with Hart Schaffner & Marx of Chicago were established, allowing them to sell under the 'Austin Reed of Regent Street' label, a factory at Lifford in Eire was opened and the headquarters moved to Thirsk in North Yorkshire, this area chosen because of its ready rail and road access to London. In 1971 a further eight shops opened, including one in Dublin.

Austin Reed bought Chester Barrie, a highly regarded suit manufacturer, which, with the most up-to-date manufacturing equipment, produced the first 'Austin Reed of Regent Street' collection of ready-to-wear suits, overcoats, jackets and trousers, all of which were being sold by Burberry, Gieves & Hawkes, Harrods and Scotch House as well as the group's own stores.

To meet the rise in women taking executive positions, in 1979 a separate women's department was opened, called 'Options'. After a couple of years' bad trading, along with the rest of the high street, Austin Reed was back to a record-breaking trading profit of nearly £4 million by 1985.

Today, Austin Reed's flagship is still its Regent Street store but there are over forty branches throughout the United Kingdom. Customers in the United States can buy Austin Reed clothes in Cashmeres of Scotland.

Bentalls

The son of a draper, Frank Bentall grew up in rural Essex. After gaining more experience in Southhampton, in 1867, Frank heard of a small draper's shop for sale in Clarence Street, in the small town of Kingston upon Thames. By the end of the first year they were averaging £200 per week.

Frank ensured the reliability of the goods and the satisfaction of the customers and expected the same of his staff. The store's 'cash only' policy kept prices low, and customers came from miles around. The premises were extended in 1878 to allow room for millinery, jackets, costumes, hosiery, fabrics, and ladies' and children's underwear; other departments specialized in clothes for mourning, as well as one selling carpeting and matting.

Of Frank Bentall's two sons, both of whom joined at this time, Leonard Hugh's vision brought great developments. Gradually the store grew and brass plates bearing its name Clarence House were raised in 1904. Electric lighting and huge plate glass

RIGHT: *Frank Bentall*
BELOW: *Frank Bentall's shop in Clarence Street, 1912*
FACING PAGE: *The famous façade of the flagship Kingston store in the 1970s*

windows added to the magnificence. A pneumatic tube system carried money in brass tubes at forty miles an hour from the counters to a central cash department. The store's reputation grew, and 'Frank Bentall, address well-known' was the advertising slogan!

Frank Bentall retired in 1909. Herbert H Perkins, from Harrods, joined and stayed for fifty years! Staff who had previously slept on the premises moved away to form the Clarence House Members' Club. Clarence Arms, the last piece in the jigsaw, was finally bought in 1919.

In 1912 the store's telephone number was changed to 'Kingston 1' and Frank accepted the fact that everyone was now calling the store simply by the name Bentalls.

Leonard Bentall bought property round the corner in Wood Street, justifying its dubious location by quoting from Emerson: 'If a man can write a better book, preach a better sermon, or make a better mousetrap than his neighbour, though he build his house in the woods the world will beat a path to his door . . . If you live long enough you will see in Wood Street one of the finest buildings in this country, and the road, one of the best in town!'

Frank Bentall died in 1923 and two years later the firm became a private limited company. For cost reasons, Bentalls decided to generate its own power and shone like a beacon whenever the rest of the town's power failed.

In 1930 the present 700-foot, five-storey store, building was designed, complete with an escalator and an air-extraction system. The final section was opened on 9 September 1935 with an hourly fanfare from four trumpeters from the Coldstream Guards.

Continual publicity campaigns were to be important, including displaying Sir Malcolm Campbell's world record-breaking car. In 1933 'The Packeteria – the shop of 1950', the first self-service café was created.

By 1936 Gerald and Rowan Bentall joined the company which was diversifying into selling motor cars as well as building houses. They gave Max Factor its first stand in the country and daily lectures were given on beauty, make-up and foot comfort.

During the war the store had its own territorial unit consisting of nearly 300 officers and men, many of whom saw active service. The company engaged a reserve group of women drivers. On 17 August 1940, the store suffered a direct hit when a string of bombs landed on the roof, destroying forty-seven pianos and setting fire to a stockroom which contained black-out material. Fortunately the damage was mainly restricted to the one floor, and there was no further damage.

Leonard Bentall died on Christmas Eve 1942. In 1946 Bentalls went public, the issue being heavily oversubscribed, and shortly after this it was discovered that the Worthing store was for sale. It had been founded in 1875 by Charles Bentall with money provided by Frank Bentall, the founder of the Kingston store, and his brother Leonard, so that Charles might live in a place that would benefit his health. Gerald and Rowan now decided to bring it into

the main company. It became their first take-over.

To help Britain recover from the war, the company started using Union Jack and 'We believe in England' stickers. In-store displays featured British craftsmen at work. When Britain staged the 1948 Olympic Games, many of the athletes stayed at Richmond Park and of course shopped at Bentalls, both in Kingston and at the Olympic camp.

In the 1950s the store's large book exhibitions were popular with authors such as Sir Mortimer Wheeler, Twiggy, Philip Harben, and Charlie the Chimpanzee, who came along with Mary Chipperfield. In 1950 and 1951, giant boards gave news of the election results.

When Gerald and Rowan's mother died in 1953, an old family Christmas pudding recipe became the basis of the Bentalls Christmas pudding, which has become such a feature of their Christmas sales.

As housing and shopping tastes have changed, so Bentalls have moved with the times. In 1973 they opened a purpose-built store in Bracknell, which had a nine-storey car park. Further developments followed in Tonbridge, Ealing and Thurrock. In 1990, the Bentall Centre was opened, with 100 shop units and a 1,200-space multi-storey car park. The company continues to live by its motto, 'To strive, to seek, to find'.

THE BODY SHOP

Anita Roddick's story, and subsequently The Body Shop, may seem to be a collection of isolated experiences and yet, as so often happens in life, a common thread exists preparing her for life's rich experiences.

Anita's mother, Gilda, came from Italy to be a nanny in England. It had been arranged for her to marry Donny Perella, even though she was in love with her cousin Henry. Although Gilda married Donny, she and Henry secretly corresponded. Reunited in Littlehampton, they had a passionate affair, resulting in the birth of Anita and her brother Bruno.

Gilda and Donny, and later Henry after their marriage in 1950, ran the Clifton Café in Littlehampton. All members of the family were expected to help, peeling potatoes or buttering endless slices of bread. Life was not easy, all the family sleeping in one room, while the other rooms were let to bring in extra money.

Already Anita was learning about business and relationships with young people. Exotic ice-cream dishes and the then little-known Coca-Cola were very popular. At school Anita supplied bubble gum and American comics that Henry had brought over, pretending new exciting editions were on their way, thus keeping up the interest and the price.

When Anita went to St Catherine's Convent school, she saw the problems of poverty. This had such a profound effect on her that one day she gave away her new school uniform to a pupil in tattered clothes. Although she failed her 11+, she later went on to train to become a teacher. At college she won a scholarship to study in Israel for three months, and although she lived in a kibbutz she found a freedom and confidence as she hitched around the country. After this she spent a year in Paris and shortly after got a job with the International Labour Organization in the Department of Women's Rights in Geneva. This was to have a major impact on her later life as she met people in the Third World.

By now Gilda had opened a night club above a butcher's shop in Littlehampton. When Anita arrived home, Gilda told her about one of her customers to whom she had shown all Anita's cards and letters.

His name was Gordon Roddick. There was an immediate rapport and although different in personality they had many things in common. Both were members of CND, tended to support the underdog and raised money for charities such as War on Want and Freedom from Hunger. Anita went to live with him and in August 1969 Justine was born. Within fifteen months, Anita was pregnant again. Hurriedly they arranged a visit to America to see friends and on the spur of the moment got married in a ceremony that lasted 'ten seconds flat', even having to borrow the wedding ring! Samantha was born in 1971.

They bought and converted a ramshackle eight-bedroomed house into a bed-and-breakfast. When the season ended, however, there was little trade, so they decided to change it into a residential hotel. They then acquired a restaurant where they first sold Italian-style food but soon found the public preferred steaks. They stamped their own personalities on the place, providing loud music and on a blackboard political messages attacking the local council; Anita chatted with the customers while Gordon organized the work behind the scenes. After three years they sold the restaurant.

Gordon had always wanted to ride a horse from Buenos Aires to New York, a 5,700-mile trek through remote and dangerous country, completely alone. For Anita it meant coping with two small children for two years single-handedly. And of course she would need money. She decided to open a shop selling cosmetic products – packaging them in different sizes and in cheap containers! She wanted to follow Tahitian women and others in the Polynesian Islands who used local, natural products. She already knew she would call it The Body Shop. It was not an original name, but one she had seen used in America 'at a place where dents were banged out of motors'.

FACING PAGE, TOP: *Anita Roddick at the Bryn Titli windfarm, Wales (Tegwyn Roberts)*
FACING PAGE, BOTTOM: *The first shop in Brighton*
RIGHT: *A selection of today's products*

They calcuated they would need a loan of £4000, using the hotel as collateral. Anita went with the children to see the bank manager, dressed in her best Bob Dylan T-shirt and jeans. When the bank manager turned her down, she was stunned. Gordon suggested that they play the bank at its own game, and he sent Anita to buy herself a smart business suit. They got an accountant friend to draw up an impressive-looking business plan and then made an appointment for them both to see the bank manager. Looking their best, Gordon handed over the plan, which the manager looked at for no more than two minutes before agreeing the loan.

Initially Anita made the products in her own kitchen but eventually she found a small manufacturing chemist to help her. She bought small plastic bottles, ones used to collect urine samples, which were cheap. Still she hadn't enough and offered to fill customers' own bottles – the start of recycling, out of necessity. Friends helped fill the bottles and write the labels, each giving details of the preparation and origins of the ingredients.

Anita felt that Brighton would be a good place for her shop, not least because it had

LEFT: *Anita at the original perfume stand*

a strong student culture. In a pedestrian precinct called Kensington Gardens, she saw a small scruffy shop. It was in a good position but it had water running down the walls. She painted the walls dark green to hide damp patches and hung larchlap fencing on the walls to hide the water. A designer created the logo for £25. Two undertakers had premises in Kensington Gardens and felt that The Body Shop might be bad for trade. They sent Anita a solicitor's letter; she told the local paper that she, a defenceless woman, was being harassed by these undertakers and the paper gave the story a centre-page spread. It got rid of the problem and another lesson had been learnt – that she didn't have to pay for advertising!

The Body Shop opened on Saturday, 27 March 1976. The day's takings were £130; Anita was euphoric. She involved everyone she could in her success, getting local art students to make posters, and continually showing concern for people.

By now Gordon had left for Buenos Aires. Business was good and she was keen to open a second shop, but once more the bank manager denied her a loan. Anita was not prepared to wait. Aidre, who helped in the shop, said her boyfriend, Ian McGlinn, would lend her the required £4000 in exchange for a half-share in the business. When The Body Shop went public, Ian's stake was worth £4 million and by 1991 it was worth in excess of £140 million. However, Anita does not regret this for Ian's money was there when she needed it.

The second, larger shop was opened in Chichester – complete with staff in uniform. On Gordon's return, they decided to expand further, yet still the banks would not lend them money. However, other branches of The Body Shop were opened, via an informal arrangement whereby the Roddicks supplied all the products. Gordon called the idea 'self-financiing'. By 1980 such shops were opening up in Europe, under tight agreements which incorporated the use of a corporate identity and the making of a premium payment.

In 1984 the company was floated. Shares reached £1.65 each and Anita had become a millionaire. She was keen to use her new position to lobby for environmental and human rights issues, which continues to be central to the company's policies. Much work has been done to alleviate the problems experienced by remote tribes, often with unique health problems, and help has been given to certain specific geographical areas where environment or economic difficulties exist. Staff in individual shops are encouraged to share in such concerns and in the campaigns that have been launched to either raise public awareness or to try to remedy the problem itself.

Anita Roddick lists her secrets of success as optimism, humanism, enthusiasm, curiosity, love, humour, magic and fun, and, most of all, euphoria. Anita may be alone in her criteria for success, but she has proved it can work!

The ancestry of the Boots family has been traced back to Richard Boote of Diseworth in Leicestershire who died in 1577. In later days the paternal ancestors of Jesse Boot (b. 2 June 1850) had lived in the small Nottinghamshire village of Willoughby on the Wolds. John Boot, Jesse's father, had grown up to be a farm labourer, but later, due to poor health, he left this and became a herbalist.

As a child, Jesse Boot accompanied his father into the woods, identifying plants for his herbal remedies. Jesse was only ten years old when his father died. He left school at thirteen and started to help his mother, Mary, full-time in their little shop, which sold soap, soda, camomile, senna, household necessities and simple herbal remedies. In any spare moments he had, Jesse would learn all he could about pharmacy.

In 1877, Jesse took control of the chemist's shop in Goose Gate, selling 'Drugs and Proprietary Articles at Reduced Prices', and introduced lines such as black lead and candles. He had worked out how he could undercut the monopoly of the 'proper' chemists who practised a price-fixing policy: he had to raise his sales to £20 a week in order to buy in large quantities and sell at low prices. He advertised in the *Nottingham Daily Express* informing readers of the 128 items he stocked from Allen's Hair Restorer to Woodhouse's Rheumatic Elixir, emphasizing their reduced prices. His tactics provoked violent opposition from other chemists. Within the first month his takings had risen to £40 a week.

Jesse Boot's aim was to attract working-class people who could now afford a few of the things he had to offer and for their benefit he also created some special offers such as soft soap at 4½*d* for 2lb, when other shops were selling it at 4*d* a 1lb. On such occasions, he would have a bell-ringer touring the streets of Nottingham which brought customers flocking to his shop. His hard

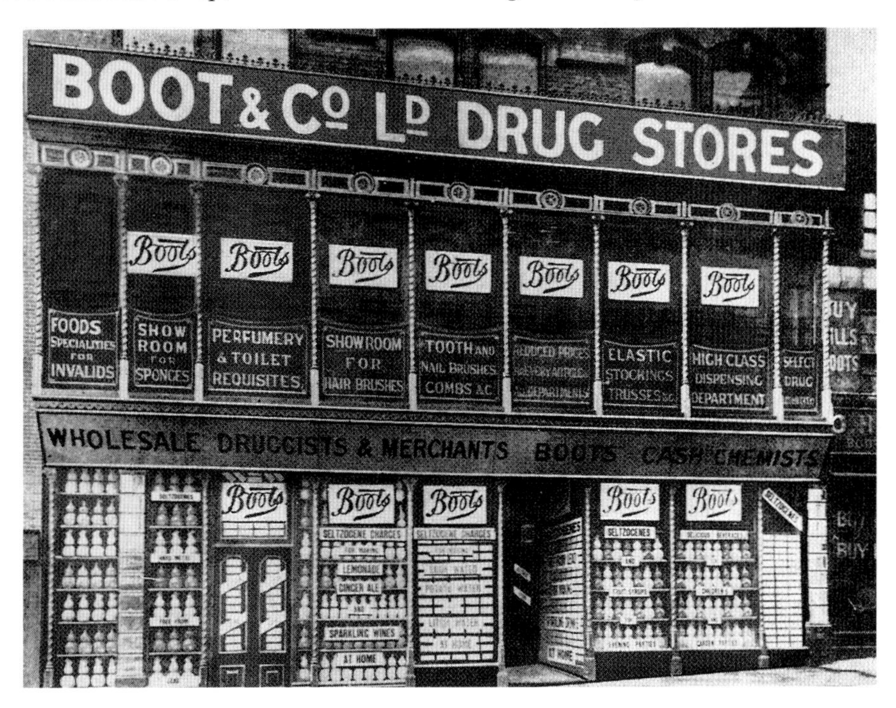

RIGHT: *Shop advertising, showing vast range of merchandise available*

LEFT: *Jesse Boot*
RIGHT: *Jesse Boot's first shop, Goose Gate, Nottingham*
FACING PAGE, TOP: *Early packaging of own-brand soap*
FACING PAGE, BOTTOM: *Toothpaste packaging*

work and concern for the poor came from his ardent Methodist upbringing and adherence to the John Wesley Primitive Physic for his folk medicine. Later he renamed his shop 'The People's Store'.

He opened splendid new premises, planned by himself, which had a plate-glass frontage, intersected by tastefully gilded and spiralling columns. There was a central office from which he could control the departments of his growing concern and also a large workshop area where Jesse's own preparations were made – the forerunner of Boots Own Brand. Doctors of his day had the monopoly of making up their prescriptions after seeing patients. Jesse engaged a young qualified chemist, E S Waring, who was also keen on prescriptions. The people initially could not take their prescriptions to the cut-price druggists as they were not incorporated, but Jesse was determined to make a breakthrough.

Eventually he won the fight and both Boot and Waring lived to see the firm handle over a million prescriptions a year, charging only half of what other chemists were asking in 1884.

Jesse Boot changed the name yet again. His chain of ten shops was now called 'Boots Cash Chemist'. Jesse raised capital from friends and J Boot & Co Ltd was formed. The long hours began to take their toll on Boot. The first shop had been kept open to 9pm on most evenings and until 11pm on Saturdays, and then there was the writing up to do after that. At stocktaking time, when he had several branches, he would work right through every night for a fortnight! So he employed a young man from Belfast named Albert Thompson to became general manager.

At the age of thirty-six, Jesse was worn out. He went to Jersey to convalesce and while he was there he met Florence Rowe, daughter of a local bookseller. They married and set up home in Nottingham. Florence was a lively person, who loved clothes and entertaining; she also had an exceptional business sense.

The company continued to expand and by 1896 they had sixty shops spread over twenty-eight towns. Still there was opposition, which led to a decree of Parliament in 1908 which stated that a qualified pharmacist had to be in attendance at each branch.

It was Florence who encouraged Jesse to devote a part of a few shops to stationery, artists' material, books and other goods. It was also her idea to start a circulating library. She knew that many people who used the shop would become bed-ridden and the long hours in bed could be better passed if they had books to read. Boots' Book-Lovers Library charged borrowers 2d per book. Of course they had to pass through the shop to get to the library counter, remembering items they needed along the way!

In 1909 Jesse received a knighthood, but illness was taking an increasing hold on his body. At the age of seventy he was ready to pass the business on but unfortunately he didn't have faith in any one successor, not even his own son John. He sold his controlling interest to an American, Louis K Liggett. At that time there were 600 Boots shops in the chain. The sale figure was £2,250,000.

In 1920 Jesse received the freedom of the City of Nottingham and was raised to the peerage as the 1st Lord Trent of Nottingham in 1929. His benevolence towards the city over the years had mounted to at least £2 million.

Jesse Boot died an invalid in 1931. Two years after his death, Florence Boot opened the 1000th Boots shop, which was in Galashiels.

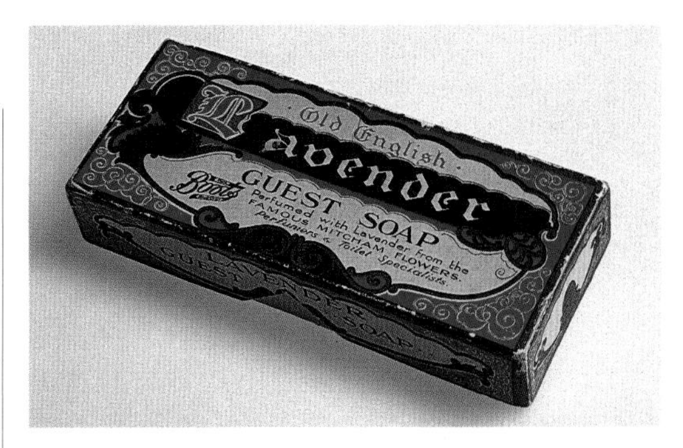

John Boot led a consortium of British financiers to successfully buy back Boots in 1933. John became the second chairman and the 2nd Lord Trent on the death of his father.

Throughout all this period, Boots was also developing as a manufacturing company. During the days of the First World War they manufactured large quantities of respirators, containing a special compound which resisted poison-gas, and they also supplied troops with over 115 million sterilizing tablets for purifying water. In the latter years of Jesse's life a 300-acre factory site had been purchased three miles south west of Nottingham, where a soap factory was built. The Boots research departments are still in the centre of Nottingham.

Today there are no members of the Boot family on the Board, but many of Jesse Boot's ideas are still present in the work that goes ahead.

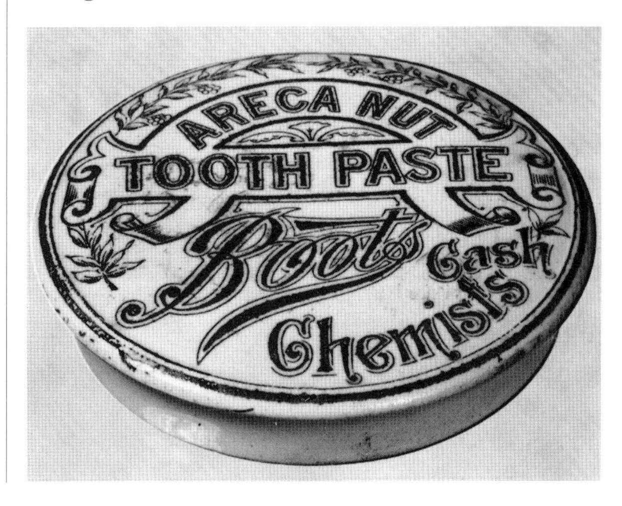

Thomas Burberry, whose father, also Thomas, a farmer, was born in either Brockham Green or Betchworth, near Dorking in Surrey in 1835. It has not been possible to confirm his birth details; perhaps his parents were Baptists, for he became one in later life, in which case no baptism entry would exist and his birth was before the introduction of civil registers.

At the age of twenty-one, Thomas opened his first outfitters shop in Winchester Street, in the then rural market town of Basingstoke, Hampshire. He was not only interested in making clothes but also in the reasons why they were worn, and indeed if they were the right type of clothing for a particular purpose. His experience on the farm would have made him aware of a shepherd's life; Burberry saw himself as a dress reformer.

In 1858, Thomas Burberry married Catherine Hannah Newman at Salem Chapel, Strand in London. They had several children, including two boys, Thomas Jnr and Arthur, both of whom joined the business.

By 1871, Burberry's shop in Basingstoke employed eighty staff. Having seen the linen smock-frocks worn by shepherds and farmers he

BELOW LEFT: *'The Burberry' – an advertisement from* Punch, *1947.*
RIGHT: *Thomas Burberry.*
BELOW: *Burberry's first shop in the Haymarket, London.*
FAR BELOW: *Burberry weatherproof for ladies in the early 1900s.*
FACING PAGE, TOP: *Burberry Gabardine tent taken by Captain Scott on his sledge journey 'Farthest South'.*
FACING PAGE, BOTTOM: *The Tielocken Burberry, one of many styles approved by the War Office between 1914 and 1918.*

realized they were cool in summer, warm in winter, easy to wear and wash, and they kept the wearer moderately dry. He also realized that their ability to keep out the wet depended on the close weave of the fabric and the loose style of the garment. Knowing that cotton could be produced more cheaply than linen, he sought the help of a local cotton-mill owner in an effort to produce the ideal waterproof cloth. After much experimenting with material used in the agricultural smock, at last success came – a superb cloth, proofed in the yarn before weaving, without the use of rubber, and then woven closely and proofed again by the same process while still in the piece. He called his cloth Gabardine, a word of old French extraction referring to a garment of cotton or silk with a woollen lining. Shakespeare knew the word, for in *The Merchant of Venice* he says, 'You spet upon my Jewish gaberdine.'

The material was completely waterproof, yet was cool and comfortable to wear. It would not tear, which made it ideal for clothing for field sports in which he had a great interest. He had already devised short coats or jackets and breeches for use by those who fished for trout or who went shooting for game. In 1888 he took out a patent for 'Improved Materials Specially Adapted for the Garments of Sportsmen'. It consisted of two materials, the outer a twill or plain linen fabric such as his Gabardine and the inner a cloth tweed which had been waterproofed or semi-waterproofed. Unlike the rubber-based treatments, Burberry's Gabardine could 'breathe', its porosity satisfying concerns expressed at the International Health Exhibition of 1884.

In 1889 the company arranged with the Jermyn Street Hotel, in London's Piccadilly, for Arthur Burberry, the younger son, to go to the hotel to meet potential customers, taking orders and giving fittings, but as orders grew they took premises at 30–35 The Haymarket. Later a warehouse and wholesale business was opened in Golden Square, supplying agents throughout the country, and in 1892 Burberry erected a mill in London Street to manufacture his cloth. He was an ardent Baptist and at the Hackwood Road work-

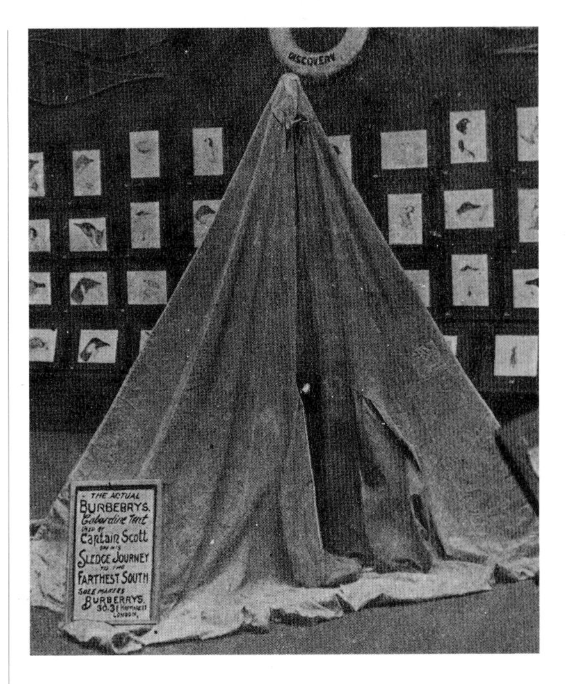

room workers would gather for a prayer meeting to begin the day. He was also generous to charities, a teetotaller, a non-smoker and a temperance worker strongly supporting Sunday closing. In addition to all these, he was a keen sportsman.

On Monday 17 April 1905, at about 6 o'clock in the morning, tragedy struck at the Basingstoke shop. We are told that Miss Gray, a millinery department assistant, was lighting up the front window, using a taper, when without warning a piece of material dropped on it and burst into flames. Another assistant tried to extinguish the flames but the fire spread, and before the fire brigade arrived the shop was an inferno. Twenty-five women lived above the shop and they lost all their belongings. The horse-drawn fire-engine had a steam pump, but it took twenty minutes to get up

LEFT: *Captain Scott's sledge*
BELOW: *The Burberry coat for men and women*

pressure on the two jets, whilst the water from the hydrant was so weak the water hardly reached the shop ceiling. £30,000-worth of damage was caused, but the store was rebuilt as an emporium.

The War Office asked Burberry to design a new service uniform for British officers; officers could place orders for their own uniform at a tailor of their choice, but now they had to be cut to Burberry's approved pattern and many started to choose Burberry as their tailor. Lord Kitchener, Lord Baden-Powell and many other famous generals adopted Burberrys and so the trend was set.

Thomas Burberry now had a country residence at nearby Hook. In 1917 he also acquired a house with large grounds, Abbots Court in Weymouth, allowing the grounds to be used for religious functions. He died in 1926 in his ninety-first year. His son Thomas died the following year, and Arthur Burberry was left to develop the business.

Burberrys' products continued to make news in the twentieth century when the company designed a tent for Roald Amundsen to use on his journey to the South Pole. After Captain Sir John Alcock made the historic first flight across the Atlantic, he wrote: 'I am writing to tell you how very satisfactory the Burberry proved . . . Although in a continual mist, rain or sleet, I kept as dry, warm and comfortable as it is possible under such conditions.' Years later, the Burberry coat was to be seen, worn by Peter Sellers, in the film, *The Pink Panther*.

Today there are Burberrys stores in Britain, France, Germany, Belgium, Switzerland and in several major cities in the United States. Royal Warrants are held from both Her Majesty the Queen and the Prince of Wales, and on five occasions Burberrys has been awarded the Queen's Award, either for Industry or for Export Achievement.

BURTON

MENSWEAR

Meshe David Osinsky was born in 1885 in the small town of Kurkel in the Kovno province of Russia, later known as Lithuania. He was educated in a village cheder until the age of thirteen and then entered the yeshiva at Slobodka, a suburb of Kovno, intending to study to become a rabbi.

Along with many other Russian Jews he fled to Britain in 1900, with, allegedly, £100 given to him by his uncle. It is likely he landed in Hull, but the only English word he knew was 'Leeds'. At that time the city was the home of about 12,000 Jews, 1,000 of those being involved in tailoring.

As a Jew, he was still likely to face persecution even in England. He minimized this by moving to Chesterfield where there would be very few Jews and there he sold flannel suits and was a pedlar selling laces. In 1904 he opened a hosier and draper's shop at 20 Holywell Street. By this time he had taken the name of Morris Burton, which he was soon to change to Montague Burton. He also had a shop by the church with the famous twisted spire and later another shop was opened in Mansfield.

His personal life was very austere, so much so that he re-used envelopes to the extent that the Post Office refused to accept them. He also queried the purchase of a 1d sheet of pins, telling staff to hammer them straight again!

Chesterfield had been a wise choice, for not only was it a busy town with a population of about 43,000, but it was also the centre for a much larger surrounding farming community and in an area where both coal mining and iron work had developed. Clothing was therefore much in demand and initially Burton bought from wholesalers cheap clothing

TOP: *Montague Maurice Burton weds Sophia Amelia Marks on 23 March 1909*
RIGHT: *Witton Street, Northwich, Cheshire*

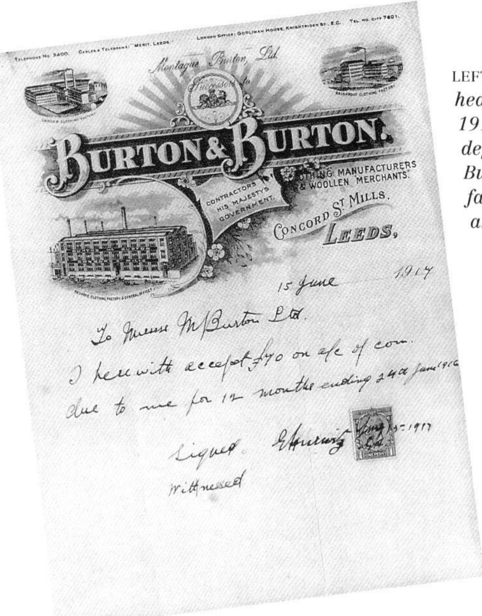
BURTON & BURTON.
CLOTHING MANUFACTURERS & WOOLLEN MERCHANTS.
CONTRACTORS TO HIS MAJESTY'S GOVERNMENT.
CONCORD ST MILLS,
LEEDS.

15 June 1917

To Messrs M Burton Ltd.

LEFT: *Letter heading from 1917 depicting Burton's factories and offices*

which he could then retail to such people.

Burton's first newspaper advertisement was in the *Derbyshire Times* on 14 April 1906, where he told prospective buyers that 'although the prices may seem low assurance is given that all the clothing offered is of a reliable quality'. The men's suits were either made of black vicuna (wild llama wool) or of brown tweed.

On 23 March 1909, Montague married Sophia Amelia Marks in Worksop. They set up home in a small terrace house in Violet Bank Road in Sheffield, and the next year he became a naturalized British citizen (although documentation still referred to him as Morris Burton).

Premises were opened at 101–3 The Moor in Sheffield in the name of Burton and Burton. He had fourteen shops in total before the outbreak of the First World War. It is believed that he was much helped in those first twenty years by the London County Westminster & Parr's Bank and also by a Mr Johnson. For most of these years, Montague was a chronically sick man suffering from a kidney disease and defective distance vision among other problems, and it was through these health problems that he missed military service.

By 1916 he was manufacturing 48,000 garments a year. The following year Burton became a limited liability company, but Montague Burton held all the shares except for one which was in his wife's name! They now employed 400 staff. The essence of his success was accuracy and speed of completing the order. The end of the First World War saw an unprecendented demand for men's suits, and with five factories in Leeds, Burton was equipped to meet that demand.

By 1939 the 595 shops spread across the country had a uniform façade; 'Burton the Tailor of Taste' was instantly recognizable in the high street.

Burton established pioneering welfare schemes and paid his workers generously. At the same time, he exhorted his shop inspectors to 'make business their hobby'. Each branch had to submit to head office a weekly account of the garments sold during the week, ensuring everything was ultimately under his control.

From as early as 1924 the company developed a massive property resource which has been a great asset, and today, with over 2000 shops in the group, the portfolio is valued at more than £1 billion.

The chairman's statement for the year ending March 1951 was Sir Montague's last. The company had become a household name. After his death a number of mergers took place to strengthen the management team. Today the group includes many well-known high street names in its ownership, including Top Shop, Top Man, Principles, Evans, Debenhams, Peter Robinson and Dorothy Perkins, the latter being named after a famous rose, which was raised in America by Jackson & Perkins.

The Brenninkmeyer family were farmers who, while living in Mettingen, a German/Dutch border town, took on Dutch nationality in the 1700s. The farm was not big enough to support all the family and so two of them, brothers Clemens and August Brenninkmeyer became travellers who sold textiles, linen and other cloths.

In 1841 Clemens and August opened a shop in Sneek in the Freisland area of the Netherlands and called it C & A, using the initials of their Christian names. Next to the shop they had a small workroom and there they made up coats, dresses and other garments. Gradually they expanded to Amsterdam, Rotterdam and other Dutch towns. While all the shops used the C & A name, they were not all owned by the two brothers, but ownership remained within the family, various members loaning money to close relatives.

In 1910 some members of the family crossed into Germany and there they repeated the pattern. Like ventures were set up in other European countries, the British one commencing in 1922 with a store on London's Oxford Street, this being known as C & A Modes. It sold 'day and evening frocks', 'charming and inexpensive garments for the little ones' and 'fur coats of wonderful value'. The formula was to offer the latest fashion at prices the general public could afford; at that time the idea was a revolution in British shopping and was coupled with very wide ranges of merchandise. Other English stores were opened in Liverpool in 1924, Birmingham in 1926 and Manchester in 1928.

In 1957 menswear was brought in and during the following decade C & A

ABOVE: *C & A Sneek, Netherlands*
BELOW: *Clemens (left) and August (right) Brenninkmeyer*

introduced the bikini and championed the mini-skirt. The Clockhouse label for young trendsetters followed and then the Westbury range for the businessman.

C & A in Britain celebrated its Golden Jubilee in 1972, at which time there were fifty-five stores. The 100th store was opened in 1985 and today there are 120.

C & A is unique in that it does not have an international headquarters, no holding or parent company, although they do all share the same formula, philosophy and high family values. C & A is not quoted on any stock exchange, individual family directors taking positions of responsibility within the companies.

Today, as distinct from their beginnings, the stores do not own any manufacturing outlet but insist that their suppliers comply with all statutory obligation and codes of practice. The products must be produced in factories where children are not exploited and where environmentally damaging processes are fully controlled.

C & A is determined that it will continue to be a company owned and operated as a family enterprize with standards strongly based on family values. The company continues to place great importance on long-term relationships and these policies very much influence corporate decision-making.

LEFT: *Advertisement in the* Daily Mail, *1922*
BELOW: *C & A, Oxford Street, London*

While Robert Owen is often regarded as the father of the Co-operative movement, the concept of co-operation goes back beyond the end of the eighteenth century.

An early example of a co-operative trading company is one established in Oldham in 1795 to arrange the bulk purchase of cheap foodstuffs.

Some of the early leaders of the movement were strongly influenced by publications sent out from the London Society for the Promotion of Co-operative Knowledge in the late-1820s. Birmingham also had an early co-operative periodical, the *Birmingham Co-operative Herald*, and during the 1830s there was much interest in the concept.

About 1830 some mechanization developed in areas near to coal mines, rivers or where there were other sources of power. Alongside the new factories terraced houses were built which often had no sanitation and opened onto the street. Several families lived in one dwelling giving much overcrowding and resultant disease. With no garden the new-town-dwellers were dependent on local shopkeepers for all their food, but often they had no money to buy it.

Wages were kept low by employing young children, sacking them when they reached a certain age. This policy led to acute poverty, the children also suffering from getting no education and often being injured at work. If the factory ran out of work, workers were sent home, without pay, until more work came in. The rich were becoming richer, the poor poorer.

The vision of a 'New System of Society' was needed. Co-operation, or socialism, as the Owenite creed was to be called relied on selfishness being replaced by brotherhood,

ABOVE: *Robert Owen*
ABOVE, RIGHT: *Toad Lane, site of first store*
RIGHT: *Fun advertisement for boot polish*

competition by unity. Its aim was to banish unemployment and poverty, ensure a fair distribution of work and wealth, provide for sickness and old age, educate children, and make all men virtuous and happy. Such communities would be rationally planned, with a proper balance between agriculture and industry. Trade would be based upon a new monetary system, labour being the source of value. Payment for work would be 'labour notes', which could be exchanged for goods in 'labour exchanges', thus giving the workers the whole produce of their labour.

Robert Owen was born at Newtown on the Welsh borders in 1771. He left school at the age of seven but by nineteen he was manager of some new large spinning mills which employed 500 workers. He was becoming a wealthy man, though he still cared for his workers.

After his marriage he became managing director of large cotton mills in New Lanark in Scotland and it was here that he was appalled to see children, some as young as five years old, being sent to work in the mill. He did much to improve conditions, giving better wages, shortening the working day, appointing health visitors, building schools and introducing new subjects to the curriculum such as music and nature study. To the surprise of other mill owners the New Lanark mills succeeded and were profitable.

Robert Owen started writing about his experiments and tried to persuade others to follow his example. There was a lot of conflict, however, among working men as to how to achieve 'the greatest happiness of all'. While Owen was in America during the 1820s, a group of working-class men started some trade associations, but Owen did not think this went nearly far enough. The first co-operative congress was held in Manchester in May 1831. The North West of England United Co-operative Company was established in Liverpool but this was a wholesale trading company making bulk purchases for retail societies and the exchange of goods manufactured in co-operatives.

The trade union movement and the co-operative movement worked very closely together but met much resistance from both employers and the government. The situation came to a climax in March 1834 when six labourers were arrested and sentenced

FACING PAGE: *The original members*
RIGHT: *Float for Oxenhope Society, early 1900s*
BELOW: *Advertisement*

to transportation for their part in attempting to form a union. As a result of such action the unions, and also the co-operative ventures, started to collapse.

Nevertheless Owen and others encouraged people to seek this higher moral way and congresses continued to be held in various parts of the country. In 1838 there was

a move to establish that every man, property owner or not, should have a vote; that Members of Parliament should be paid, thus allowing poor men to sit in Parliament; that voting should be in secret; and that there should be an election every year. The advocates of such a cause became known as the Chartists, but it was in 1841 that Owenites became known as Socialists.

In Rochdale, Lancashire, a group of working men started a scheme to gather as much money as they could to buy and sell basic commodities collectively. Among them were Charles Howarth, a warper in a cotton mill, and James Smithies, a wool-sorter. For many months they gathered together what little money they could, but how could they ensure that their customers would stay faithful to them? Charles Howarth suggested that the profits be divided among the members in proportion to how much they spent in the store. This 'dividend' was to become most important for in many families it was used to buy shoes and other necessities for the children. The group became known as the Rochdale Society of Equitable Pioneers, the society being established on 15 August 1844.

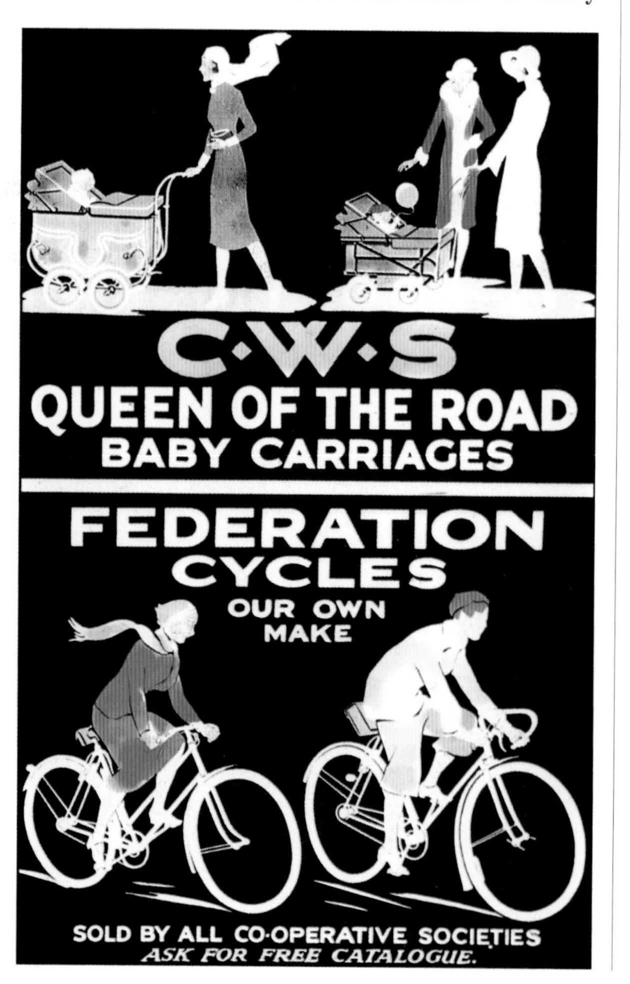

The objectives of the new society were many and far-reaching for their time. They included the establishment of a store, building or purchasing houses to improve members' social and domestic conditions, manufacturing articles thereby providing employment for members who were without work, establishing a self-supporting home colony, and, for the promotion of sobriety, opening a temperance hotel in one of the society's houses.

The twenty-eight original pioneers included weavers, a shoemaker, a blockprinter, a hatter and a hawker. They had little money and at first had great difficulty finding a place to open their stores, finally renting the ground floor of an old warehouse underneath a chapel – it was in Toad Lane, Rochdale. They opened for business on 21 December 1844, then opening two evenings a week from about 8–10pm. At first takings varied from £4–7 each week, but sales gradually increased. New members had to be proposed and seconded by two members and had to buy four £1 shares in the society, which could be paid in instalments. However, far more than £4 would be returned in the form of dividend on his purchase, so he saved £4 without really noticing.

As the years passed other departments opened and an education committee estab-

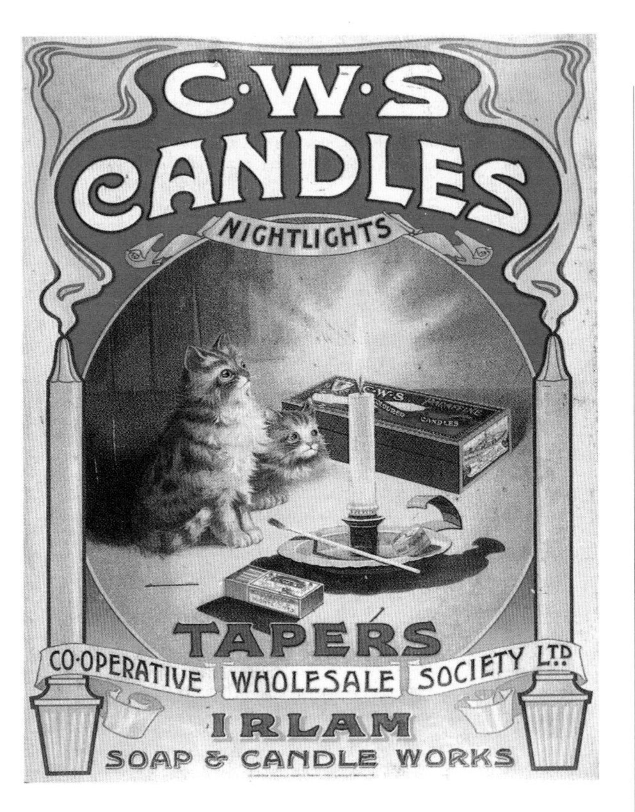

lished. By 1849 they had 390 members and the capital sum had risen to £1193. The first branch was opened in 1856 in Oldham Road, Rochdale. In 1862 they achieved another of their plans by building their first eighteen cottages for members to live in. Co-operation started to spread further afield and proved it really could work.

The Co-operative Wholesale Society came into existence in 1863 in a small warehouse in Manchester. In 1873 they started to manufacture goods: biscuits, boots and shoes, soap, and, later, washing machines and wringers, bedsteads and mattresses, and even a corset-making factory. Towards the end of the century they bought estates totalling 813 acres in Ceylon for tea production and in Denmark they acquired a butter depot at Esbjerg.

Over the years Co-operative Societies have grown up to span the country. Today the co-operative movement has about 4600 shops, including seventy-six superstores, some of which operate with turnovers which other retailers would not consider worthwhile, but the Co-op sees such trading as a service to the community. Another trading area is the funeral service, which conducts about twenty-five per cent of funerals in Britain. Other significant areas of trading include the Co-operative Insurance Society and the Co-operative Bank.

ILLUSTRATIONS: *Advertisements dating between 1920–40, showing vast range of products*

The Debenham family traces its ancestry back to the village of Debenham in Suffolk to at least 1165.

William Franks, a draper, sold expensive cloth, ribbons, bonnets, gloves and fashionable parasols from his premises at 44 Wigmore Street in London. There had been a shop on those premises since 1778, and as the area became more wealthy so his trade grew. Franks formed a partnership with a man called Flint, who had probably been trained by Franks, and Flint in his turn went into partnership with Thomas Clark.

In 1813 Clark was introduced to young William Debenham, who offered to invest £500 in an equal partnership. Debenham, however, had much more to contribute to the partnership than money, having worked in the City and also for Morley, a well-known hosiery company in Nottingham. He also had connections with George Courtland, who ran a silk-throwing mill in Essex.

During this rapid period of change, London's West End was alive with the rich and successful. Profits of Clark & Debenhams, however, were to come from a different source, namely a family-mourning service. In earlier times formal mourning had been mainly restricted to court circles, but now family-mourning had become a ritual for those lower down the social echelon. The sale of suitable materials became very profitable.

At this time the new rich, those involved in industry and commerce, were seen as potential customers. Towns outside London were beginning to develop and travellers were supplying provincial shops in Chester, Harrogate and Cheltenham, enabling them to compete with London stores. It was therefore quite a breakthrough when Debenham opened a shop on the Promenade at Cheltenham, a replica of his London store. The premises were vested in Clement Freebody, who became a partner in 1851, along with William Debenham Jnr, and the firm became Debenham and

LEFT: *44 Wigmore Street, London*
FACING PAGE, TOP: *William Debenham*
FACING PAGE, BOTTOM: *Notice to all staff, 1854*

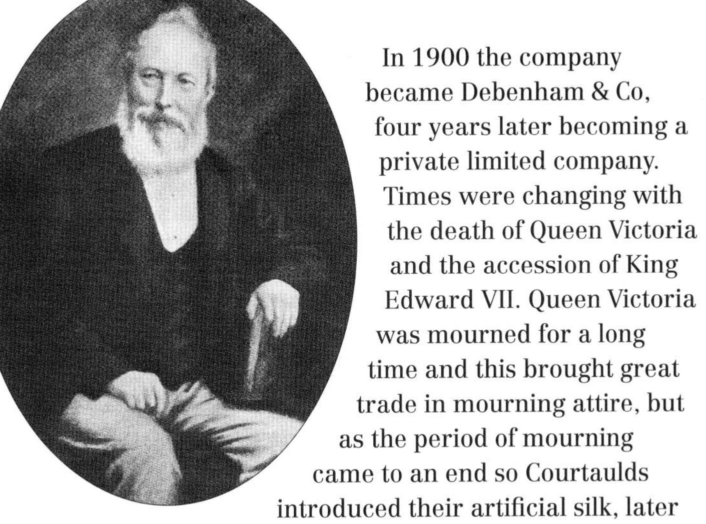

Freebody, although in Cheltenham it traded as Cavendish House, after the Cavendish family.

Both William Debenham and Clement Freebody died within a period of six years and so the business passed into the hands of William Jnr and his younger brother Frank. As William Jnr had no children it was Frank's son, Ernest Ridley Debenham, who provided the succession.

Frank began selling small quantities of cloth at reduced rates to dressmakers as well as lengths of cloth to show their clients. As a result dressmakers flocked to London, but also because it was known that at their shop the best and latest goods were always available, including those from Belgium, France and Italy. Machine-knitted garments were now being made in Leicester and Nottingham, and this lead to the production of woollen underwear made in factories. Another innovation was the creation of the Jersey, a one-piece woollen trunk with sleeves, originally a garment worn by peasants in Jersey.

Gradually the company took over other retailers, increasing their range of merchandise. As the wholesale and export aspects of the firm continued to grow, offices were eventually opened in many countries, including South Africa, Australia, Canada and even China. In England, Harrods, Selfridges and Bentalls were all customers of their wholesale departments. While to the outsider it might have looked that Debenham & Freebody were sacrificing the retail trade to these companies, in reality they were generating resources ready for a counter-attack.

In 1900 the company became Debenham & Co, four years later becoming a private limited company. Times were changing with the death of Queen Victoria and the accession of King Edward VII. Queen Victoria was mourned for a long time and this brought great trade in mourning attire, but as the period of mourning came to an end so Courtaulds introduced their artificial silk, later known as rayon. In 1903 when the Post Office was allocating its first business telephone numbers, Debenhams was allocated the premier number 'Mayfair 1', the envy of all their rivals.

In 1905 the company was registered as Debenham Limited with a capital of

NOTICE

To Shop Assistants

STORE MUST OPEN PROMPTLY
at 6.0 a.m. *until* 9.0 p.m. *all the year round.*

STORE must be swept, counter, base shelves and showcases dusted. Lamps trimmed, filled and chimney cleaned, pens made, doors and windows opened.

A PAIL of water and scuttle of coal must be brought in by each clerk before breakfast, if there is time to do so and attend customers who call.

Any employee who is in the habit of
SMOKING SPANISH CIGARS, GETTING SHAVED AT A BARBER'S SHOP, GOING TO DANCES, AND OTHER SUCH PLACES OF AMUSEMENT

will surely give his employer reason to be suspicious of his INTEGRITY and alround HONESTY

Each employee must pay not less than ONE GUINEA per year to the Church, and attend Sunday School every Sunday.

MEN are given one evening a week for courting purposes and two if they go to prayer meetings regularly.

After 14 hours work, spare time should be devoted to reading good literature.

1864

£750,000. No capital was offered to the public, but a profit-sharing arrangement benefited directors and staff. Now they had to win back the wealthy customers who responded to the 'snob' value of stunning presentation gowns and exclusive fashions that would set them apart at garden parties and other special functions. Soon they were to win the patronage of King Edward VII and Queen Alexandra, as well as the Prince and Princess of Wales.

A new image called for new buildings. The Wigmore Street store exuded luxury from the moment the customer entered its marble entrance hall. There was even an air-purification system. As quality colour-printing and engraving techniques developed, so stores produced exquisitely designed mail-order catalogues.

1914 saw the start of the First World War, a time when class distinctions were much reduced, when luxury was replaced by necessity. Textile Securities established a working relationship between Marshall & Snelgrove and Debenhams with the same buying policies and management reforms. The actual merger did not take place until 1919, this being quickly followed by the purchase of Harvey Nichols of Knightsbridge.

As peace returned, so Debenhams assumed a larger concern for staff welfare, for instance, pioneering a dental health service and, with the help of the Shop Assistants' Union, encouraging staff to take further education.

The 1920s also saw the beginning of the January sales. Shop-lifting and bad debts followed, but Debenhams were not afraid to 'blacklist' people who passed bad cheques.

As unemployment bit in the 1920s, so many department stores were finding life hard. Clarence Hatry formed the Drapery and General Investment Trust and called on member firms to subscribe £2 million, investing the money and allocating funds for redevelopment. Towards the end of 1926 Debenham Securities was formed and now Ernest Debenham became chairman. Public money was raised to finance the rearrangement of the shareholdings. A year later a scheme was sealed whereby Debenhams bought not less than seventy-five per cent of Drapery Trust shares at 30s, plus a commission of 1s 4d on each share for Hatry. The whole deal was extremely complex and saw the end of any family involvement after over a century of control. Eventually Debenhams Ltd acquired 99.8% of the issued Ordinary capital of the Drapery Trust for £2,300,000

FACING PAGE: *Reception dress with gun-metal embroidery, 1909*
RIGHT: *Modern store*

thus ensuring the future of the new departmental empire. However, Hatry's devious dealings would still cause problems, not least because the stores spread across the country had little in common, and had a total of 15,000 staff who had both varied management skills and varying levels of motivation.

In January 1934 steps were taken to remove a large amount of unremunerative capital and at last profits started to rise. In 1937 the coronation gave an opportunity for commercial exploitation with many souvenirs being produced for sale. Although the main London stores were the flagships, the profits came from provincial centres. Staff were extremely loyal, men often receiving a cheque for fifty years' service.

After the war, filling the shops with stock was very difficult and buyers and managers had to use all their skill and ingenuity to find the right item. Postwar housewives wanted easy-care colourful fabrics – a new shopping revolution was on its way.

In 1950, in the first Census of Distribution, Debenhams was shown to be the largest departmental store group with eighty-four companies and a total of 110 stores, although complete central buying was not instigated until 1966. 1950 saw the start of a long and ultimately unsuccessful battle for ownership of House of Fraser with Harrods who had already bought some Debenhams stores in Scotland. In 1966 Cresta fashion shops provided the group with fifty-one retail outlets and food and restaurant services. Stores showing continuing disappointing profits were closed.

In 1970 the management accounting guru, Sir Anthony Burney, was brought into the company and the decline in profits was reversed in his first year. However, in 1972 Bernard Lyons, chairman of the United Drapery Stores, called to announce that his company was making a takeover bid of £114 million. For two months the battle raged, but eventually UDS conceded defeat. The fight had unified staff.

Succeeding years saw other household names come into the group, including Bubsy's of Bradford, Greens camera shops, and Rayne shoe shops. Today all the stores trade under the name of Debenhams with the exception of Brown's of Chester.

In August 1985 Sir Ralph Halpern, then Chairman of the Burton Group, launched a successful bid for the sixty-five stores and Debenhams became part of the Burton Group PLC. Today, the number of stores has grown to eighty-eight, making it the largest departmental store group in Britain.

DOLLOND & AITCHISON

When King Louis XIV revoked the edict of Nantes, which had given equal legal status to Protestants and Catholics, Jean Dollond and his wife planned their escape from Normandy to England. They settled in Spitalfields in east London, home to silk-weavers. They had a son, John, born on 10 June 1706.

The London Mathematical Society was formed in 1717 and young John joined it soon afterwards, being particularly interested in Optics, a branch of Physics embracing the properties and phenomena of light. He and his wife Elizabeth had two sons, Peter born in 1731 and John Dollond II born in 1733, but family responsibilities did not diminish John's interest in Optics, exchanging theories and arguments with people round the world. He was particularly friendly with John Bird, an instrument maker in the Strand.

Peter too decided to try his fortune in the field of Optics, opening up a small business in Vine Street, Spitalfields. Two years later, he was joined by his father and they entered a formal deed of partnership. Dollond & Son then moved to the Strand, trading at the sign of the Golden Spectacles and Sea Quadrant.

John started work improving the design of the heliometer, an instrument originally used to measure the diameter of the sun, then later the angular distance between two stars. The Dollond micrometer of 1753 provided astronomers with a new and powerful means of finding the distance of the sun. Even Captain Cook used one on his voyage to Australia in 1769. As business flourished, Peter Dollond, now described as an optician (the first time the title had been used in England), took on John Berge as his apprentice, and John developed the achromatic lens (one that would not show fringes) for which he was granted a patent – bringing both prosperity and praise. His three-foot long telescopes performed as well as forty-five-foot long ones constructed by older methods. The Royal Society awarded him its highest award, the Copley Medal, in 1758 and made him a fellow three years later.

LEFT: *Eyeglasses advertisement from 1901*

FACING PAGE: *James Aitchison*

A year before his premature death in 1761, he was appointed Optician to King George III.

Peter Dollond followed his father as Optician to his Majesty and to His Royal Highness The Duke of York. As well as making achromatic telescopes, they sold tubular magnifying glasses for reading, microscopes, sextants, sundials and spectacles. Research continued and, by combining three lenses, he was soon producing telescopes which were regarded as marvels of the age. He was being spoken of as 'the Father of Practical Optics'. The slang word for telescope was 'a dollond'.

In 1766 Peter Dollond bought 59 St Paul's Churchyard and entered into a partnership with his brother John Dollond II, already a fully qualified and imaginative optician.

Three times Peter Dollond became Master of the Worshipful Company of Spectacle Makers, and it has also been suggested that he made bifocal lenses in 1781, three years ahead of Benjamin Franklin, the American scientist credited with their invention.

Whilst in Elizabethan times the wearing of spectacles had been regarded as a sign of old age, later the sale of spectacles became an important part of the Dollonds' business. They also made the fashionable spy-glasses which were taken to the opera.

In 1804 they advertised details of spectacles which had been prepared in a new way; they were referred to as Periscopic spectacles, being designed to give a wider field of view by making the objects appear distinct through all parts of the glasses. William Hyde Wollaston, their inventor, had entrusted their sole manufacture to Peter Dollond. John Dolland II died the same year.

The following year Peter Dollond had a special customer. It was Admiral Lord Nelson, who bought a telescope before going to join the *Victory* to fight the fleets in France and Spain.

Peter and John had daughters but no sons. However, their young sister, Susan, had two sons, the younger of whom, George, was a master instrument maker. It was agreed that he should take the place of John Dollond in the firm but, realizing that the Dollond name in Optics would die on the departure of Peter Dollond, it was agreed that George would change his name by deed poll.

After Peter Dollond's death, George was appointed Optician to King George IV and also Optician to his Royal Highness The Duke of Gloucester, and Mathematical Instrument Maker to the Honourable Board of Customs. He successfully applied for a Royal Charter for the Astronomical Society, a society for which he had an abiding passion.

George Dollond also had no sons but his nephew also George changed his name to Dollond. When George Dollond II became principal of the firm it was in a very prosperous state. He was appointed Optician to Queen Victoria and given the task of fitting out the royal yacht with the appropriate optical and nautical instruments. George died in 1866 and, while he was succeeded by his son William, this was then to be the end of 120 years of control by the Dollond family. William Dollond sold the business to a former employee and the firm moved to larger and better-equipped premises at 1 Ludgate Hill. This was the period of the development of photography and at a later stage this was of significant importance to the company.

Meanwhile James Aitchison was born in London in 1860, the son of Scottish parents. He was apprenticed to a firm of opticians in High Holborn, but in 1889 he set up his own business at 47 Fleet Street. The wearing of 'glasses', as they were now commonly known, had become fully acceptable and Aitchison made glasses that he could fit and sell at 2s 6d a pair, and some even for a shilling. Now they were in a price range that most people could afford, although he also offered frames created in gold or silver and, of course, monocles.

At this time anyone could put a sign over his door, carry out a few basic tests and claim to be an optician. Aitchison strongly believed that those who called themselves opticians should have earned the title and thereby the public could be assured that the optician was trained and qualified.

At the end of the nineteenth century the Strand was one of the best-known streets in the world. It was the centre of business, politics and entertainment. Aitchison opened his third practice at 428 Strand in 1895.

Aitchison advertised his sight-testing practice and products in the press, a practice much frowned upon by his fellow practitioners who considered it unprofessional. However, one competitor was advertising a recent innovation, 'Spectacles for Horses'. The idea was that horses like humans could suffer from myopia (short sight) and this could make them shy away from objects which suddenly came into view and could not be seen from a distance. An oculist could prescribe deep saucer-shape glasses, which could be fitted into bosses of leather and these completely covered the horse's eye, held inside blinkers by thin straps.

In 1905 Aitchison opened his first provincial branch in Leeds, but by 1910 his health was deteriorating rapidly and on 22 December 1911 he died suddenly at the age of fifty-one.

In 1912 the family business became a limited company. Enamel signs on railway stations and London buses were used to promote the company, showing the Owl trademark with the slogan 'Are your eyes right? If not consult Aitchison & Co.'

The period following the First World War was not easy for either company. Dollond's resorted to mail-order selling and widened their operation to include the sale of gramophone records, and even perambulators – as a company they had strayed far from their roots as maker of optical instruments.

Harold Parsons, of Dollond's, and Irvine Aitchison met in 1926 and on 31 August 1927 Aitchison & Co acquired the goodwill, leases and stock of Dollond & Co. To demonstrate his leadership of the new company Irvine called it Aitchison & Dollond. However, from a promotional point of view, it was

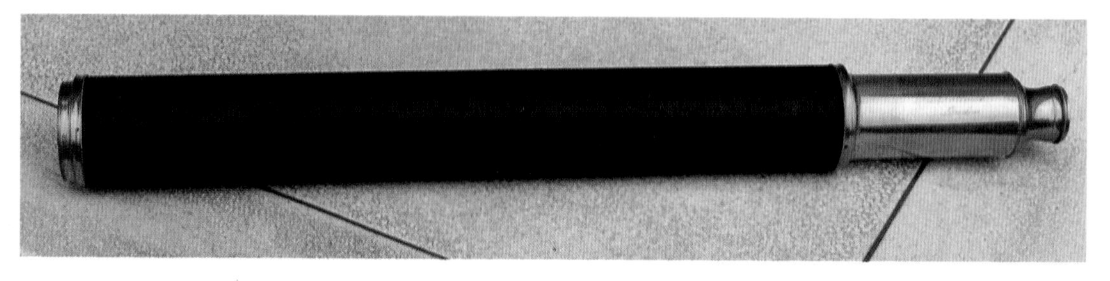

FACING PAGE: *Dollond Naval Telescope, c. 1750*
RIGHT: *Peter Dollond I*

pointed out that Aitchison was difficult to pronounce and he agreed to swap the names round.

After the Second World War the Labour Government introduced the National Health Service and now both eye tests and spectacles could be had without charge. Many people who had not previously worn glasses suddenly came forward.

Irvine Aitchison's only son, Peter, died in 1947, ending any hope of keeping the company in the family, and in December 1953 Dollond & Aitchison became a public company quoted on the Stock Exchange.

In 1962 Irvine sold a large number of shares to Television Wales and West, effectively placing them in control. In 1964 they purchased the remainder and appointed Lord Derby as chairman; Irvine Aitchison was its first president until his death in 1965.

In November 1970 the firm was acquired for £10 million by Gallaher Ltd, the tobacco enterprize, but a company with a wide spectrum of interests. Two people who had tried to guide the company, Dick Harris who came in after TWW bought the company, and Cyril Howell who had joined in 1936, were to be the chairman and deputy chairman.

In preparation for Britain's entry into the EEC it was decided to form Dollond International Ltd. In the 1970s, overseas developments actually took place in both Holland and Italy with a further development involving thirty-two branches taking place in Spain in 1982.

In 1995 there was a management buy-out, in conjunction with venture capitalists, and it is now a private company.

Today Dollond & Aitchison are to be found in most towns and cities throughout the country, being easily recognizable by the Owl sign. Things have changed a lot since John and Peter Dollond set up shop at the sign of the Golden Spectacles and Sea Quadrant.

John Beale was born in Tiverton, Somerset, just after D-Day. As a child he was brought up in a school environment, as his father was a school bursar. Later John studied Chemistry at Oxford University, then worked for Shell International in Holland and Belgium. This was an important phase in John's life when his interest in business and marketing took a major step forward, leading to his obtaining a Masters in Business Administration at Columbia University in New York. He also became involved with CBS Radio, helping set up a publishing division.

John enjoyed life in America, but now, a married man with two young boys, he decided to return to Britain. In America there had been many new ideas to be involved with, among them Creative Playthings, an organization which sold educational toys. His interest was kindled by having two boys, but also by his family's involvement in education, and now his sister had become an educational psychologist.

He had thought of becoming a teacher but now, back in England, wanted to put his business training into practice. Educational development among pre-school children in the British Isles was largely neglected, but now, as more mothers wished to follow a career, so pre-school playgroups developed and childcare became a prime concern. Similarly, at this stage, educational toys were rather limited, there being Lego and Meccano; specialists were limited to Galts and Abbatts (whose family had owned Abbatts Persuaders – makers of school canes!). Other toys were either mainly adult-orientated and expensive toys or cheap, plastic ones.

John Beale gathered round him, in Reading, a group of experts concerned with children's early development. They included Elizabeth Matterson, an early chairman of the Pre-School Playgroup Association; Mary Franklin, the head of nursery education in Reading; Betty Root of Reading University, and a nursery and primary head teacher. Together they considered the needs of young children and how educational toys could stimulate and encourage the development of young lives.

John's first project was a mail shot. The pack contained a newsletter and encouraged parents to 'sign up', giving the age of their children. Parents were then sent specialist information geared to that age. Gradually the pack became a catalogue, which was sub-divided into areas such as reading and writing, pretend-play, and others. An office was set up in an attic but in 1974 John opened his first shop in London Street, Reading.

The name over the shop was simply 'Early Learning Centre', which is an Americanism for a pre-school centre. John's concept was that it would be a place to buy toys which had educational value, but also where professional advice was available. Based on a nursery school in style, with tough carpet

FACING PAGE: *First Early Learning Centre, Reading*
RIGHT: *Children in designated play area*

on the floor, a play area where children could try out the toys, natural woods on the walls, the rule was that children *could* touch anything in the shop. In addition, at least one member of the staff at any one time would be either a nursery nurse or a nursery school teacher. The merchandise was different from usual toys shops. For instance, no guns were allowed, and everything had to be extremely tough. John would deliberately drop representatives' sample toys to test their durability. Excess packaging and gender stereotyping was also strongly discouraged.

These early days were not easy for it was the time of the three-day week and power was restricted. On some occasions lighting came from a lamp on a pole attached to a car battery! In 1976, they moved to the Kings Road and slowly business grew. In 1977 a second shop was opened and the following year John opened a branch in Bristol. He soon learned that, although the Bristol site was bigger than the previous two, it did not yield higher sales. The first fifty shops were set in secondary locations where rental was lower, but sites were chosen within 200 yards of Marks & Spencer. Still the catalogues were used, and now it also served to advertise the shops.

Under-capitalization was still a major difficulty and so, in order to aid expansion, in 1981 John sold a major stake in the company to Fine Art Developments who were very interested in the mail-order aspect of the business. The headquarters had been moved to Swindon in 1980 and the subsequent capital allowed the firm to open more shops. Rapid expansion during the next three years included the opening of nearly 100 new shops in a deliberate policy to avoid any competition setting up. Some tried, like Offspring, owned by Robert Maxwell, but when it started losing money Maxwell offered it to John Beale. John turned it down – although he poached their general manager, Ian Duncan, now chief executive of Early Learning Centre – and Offspring closed down.

As the company grew, prime high street and shopping centre locations were chosen for new sites. John also developed a strong management team, among whom was Andrew Crankshaw, Early Learning Centre's managing director.

In 1984 John Beale sold the rest of his shares to Fine Art Development, but remained with the company for a further year.

In 1985 Fine Art Developments sold the Early Learning Centre to the present owners John Menzies who have further developed it so that now there are about 180 shops spread throughout Great Britain and in Eire and Holland.

John Beale is now running Past Times, which he founded in 1986, which already has fifty shops throughout the United Kingdom and also operates an extensive mail-order business. But, of course, that's another story!

FORTNUM & MASON

ESTABLISHED 1707

The first known Fortnum, actually spelt Fortanon, was Nicholas, an Oxfordshire yeoman farmer in 1273. However, it wasn't until after the Great Fire of London that we find a Fortnum, spelt Fortnam, in London – William was a builder in Stepney and was joined there by his cousin, William Fortnum, in 1705.

William Fortnum lodged with Hugh Mason at Mason's small shop in St James's Market. In 1707 William became a footman in the Royal Household of Queen Anne, creating a link with the Royal Family which has continued without a break to the present day.

One of the 'perks' of being a footman was that he received the used candles at the end of the day. He would then sell these to the ladies of the Household for their own personal use. He was so encouraged by the success of his used-candle business that he persuaded Hugh Mason to join him as a partner in setting up a grocery 'shop', probably a stall set up in a doorway in Piccadilly, but on the site of the present building.

William continued as a footman at the Palace and put his connections to good use. Great private establishments sprang up around St James's Palace and of course they all needed the goods that William and Hugh were selling. As business boomed, so Mason's stables accommodated the increase in carriages and horses. William Fortnum concentrated on the groceries.

ABOVE: *A London landmark since 1964, this handsome clock featuring Mr Fortnum and Mr Mason adorns the shop's front entrance.*
LEFT: *View of Fortnum & Mason from Piccadilly, in 1837*
FACING PAGE: *Advertisement from Coronation year, 1953*

In 1761 Charles Fortnum, William's grandson, entered the service of Queen Charlotte, and in addition to his wage he received candles, food, coals, house-linen and wine. Through his fellow servants he also was able to introduce more business to the family concern. For nineteen years, Charles Fortnum guided the business before selling it to his son, Richard, and John Mason – Richard had seventy-five per cent of the share. At this stage Charles had been recalled to the Palace to become the Page of the Presence, an equivalent to an Equerry or Private Secretary. Three years later he was promoted to Groom of the Chamber.

Fortnum & Mason was no ordinary grocer. As early as 1788 they were selling boned portions of poultry and game in aspic jelly, decorated with lobsters and prawns; potted meats; hard-boiled eggs in forcemeat (Scotch eggs); brandy-soaked cake with whipped cream; mince pies; savoury patties and dried and fresh fruits.

Wellington's hungry officers called upon Fortnum & Mason to refresh their palates. New clubs such as the Athenaeum, Crockford's and the Garrick all served Fortnum & Mason delicacies.

They were also the first shop in London to stock Horlicks and Baxters soups. Tinned items were now becoming available, complete with opening instructions. 'To open the canister, first stab a hole with the butt-end of a knife, near the upper rim. Then insert the blade as far as it will go. Draw the handle towards you and the blade will be found to cut through the tin with perfect ease'!

One June morning in 1886, Mr Heinz arrived at Fortnum & Mason from America. He brought with him five cases of his products, ones he felt would appeal to the English taste. He showed his goods, bracing himself for the reply. The now famous

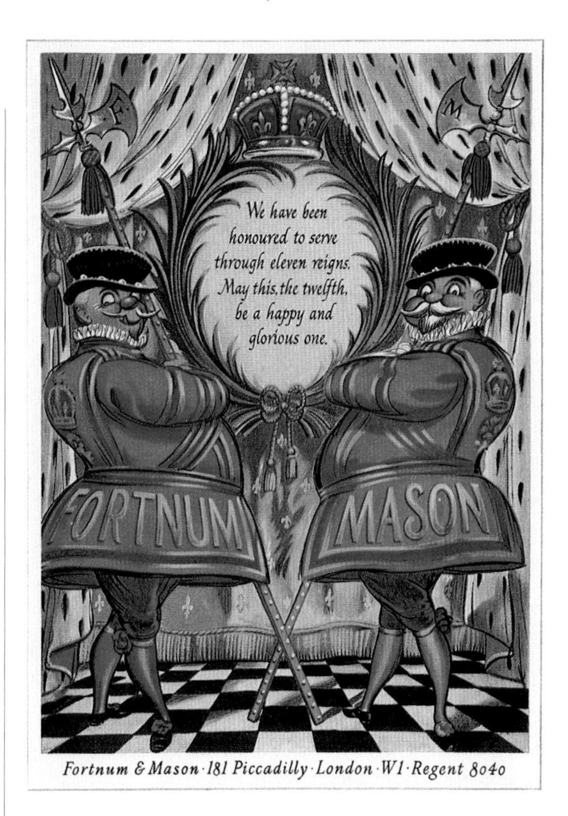

Fortnum & Mason · 181 Piccadilly · London · W1 · Regent 8040

response, 'We will take them all', meant a turning-point in Heinz's fortunes.

Fortnum & Mason celebrated its 250th anniversary in 1957. In 1964 Piccadilly acquired a magnificent new clock over the store's main door. It was the largest timepiece to be built since Westminster's Big Ben in 1861. On each side of the clock are hinged doors, which open at every hour, and through these doors appear the figures of Mr Fortnum and Mr Mason, each about four feet high. As the clock chimes they move forward, turn towards each other and bow. At the end of the chime an eighteenth-century air is played on seventeen bells, the two figures bow to each other once again and return to their respective pavilions.

Today it is still possible to buy caviar or Champagne truffles, have horseradish sauce sent out to Saudi Arabia, chocolate digestives to Zimbabwe or a Christmas lunch sent out to Nigeria.

FOYLES

William Foyle was a successful wholesale grocer. His two sons, William and Gilbert, however, opted for the Civil Service. In 1904 they failed their examinations and decided to sell their unwanted textbooks by placing an advertisement in an educational journal. The advertisement brought so many replies that the brothers decided that the book trade could be their new way forward. Within a year, they had moved to Cecil Court in Charing Cross Road. In 1906 another move took them to their present-day premises and they started selling new books, soon gaining the reputation of being able to supply any book.

William Foyle was renowned for his publicity ideas and as a result was now famous. The Lord Mayor opened Trefoile House, his new premises, which had thirty miles of shelving, with a capacity for four million books.

Foyles has a wide range of customers from abroad. Famous people who have shopped at Foyles in the ninety years of trading include Sir Noël Coward, George Bernard Shaw, Michael Jackson, Sir David Frost, Sean Connery and the Queen of Siam. Even Walt Disney found the range of art books fascinating and Noël Coward found inspiration for *Cavalcade* on the shelves at Foyles.

Anther aspect of the Foyles business is its lecture agency which was acquired by them in 1944 and includes among its speakers for luncheon clubs, literary societies and other gatherings, Godfrey Talbot, Edna Healey and Phil Drabble. Foyles Literary Luncheons

THE WORLD'S GREATEST BOOKSHOP

FOYLES

FOR BOOKS

Depts. for Books on Agriculture, Horticulture, Philosophy, Religion, Politics, and all other subjects. Stock of 4 million volumes.

119-125 CHARING CROSS ROAD LONDON WC2

QUICK POSTAL SERVICE

are held at the Grosvenor House Hotel and speakers have included Margaret Thatcher, H G Wells, General de Gaulle and Emperor Haile Selassie. Foyles even has its own publishing subsidiary, John Gifford Ltd, while another is Foyles Antiquarian Books which trades under the name of Beeleigh Abbey Books in Essex.

Today the firm is controlled by Christina Foyle, one of three children of William Foyle. A bizarre paying system is still in place: a customer brings the book or books he wants to buy to a counter and in return receives a docket; he then takes the docket to the cash register and pays the amount stated, before returning to the counter with his stamped docket to collect his books. Foyles is still the home for the elusive book; the Mecca of book-lovers from around the world.

FACING PAGE, TOP: *Beeleigh Abbey, Maldon, Essex*
FACING PAGE, BELOW: *William Foyle*
RIGHT: *Christina Foyle*

Gieves & Hawkes

Melchisadek Meredith claimed to have come to Portsmouth from Wales and to have descended from a family of princes. Certainly he had the presence of a nobleman and became known as 'Old Mel' or 'The Great Mel'. He opened a tailor's in Portsmouth – an ideal town with its links with the Royal Navy. To his good fortune, the Navy was at the time standardizing its uniforms, and Nelson was among their regular customers. Mel had such a love of uniforms that he requested on his death to be laid out dressed in his Militia Dragoons uniform!

Mel left a flourishing business, although also a large amount of debt. Instead of becoming a doctor as he had intended, Mel's only son, Augustus Hermston Meredith, entered the business to support his mother and repay debts. Eventually he lost interest and sold the business to

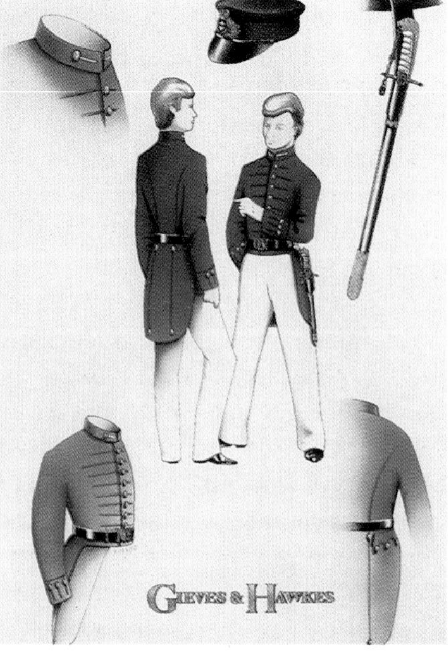

TOP: *No 1 Savile Row, London, the flagship store, originally built in 1732*
FAR LEFT: *Lord Nicholas Windsor in the pages' uniform on the occasion of the Royal Wedding, 1981*
NEAR LEFT: *Designer's sketch for the pages' uniform and accessories*
FACING PAGE: *United States Navy price list, 1935*

another Portsmouth tailor, Joseph Galt. This merger brought with it many Army and civic customers and a better standard of management.

In 1852 James Gieve joined Galt. Gieve came from a family of Huguenot refugees, who had settled in the West Country. Soon after his arrival they fitted out a large yacht as part-tailor's workshop and part-amenity ship, and, filled with the necessities of life, it set sail for the Crimea. It was a most successful venture and increased the firm's prestige as well as its profits. Their partnership lasted thirty-five years until 1887 when Gieve became the sole owner, and the firm was called Gieve & Co.

James Gieve, a respected member of the local community, being both an alderman and a Justice of the Peace, died in 1888 and was followed in the business by his sons James Watson Gieve and John Gieve.

At the turn of the century the Navy once again went through a period of extensive growth and this led to further expansion and the opening of new outlets. James Gieve forged a link with the Royal Naval College on the Isle of Wight. Gieve & Co would send telegrams of congratulations to successful candidates, followed by a visit to discuss the requirements of the College with the cadet and his parents. Such was the success of this and other policies that, over the eighteen years the College was open, no less than ninety-eight per cent of the cadets were 'dressed' by Gieve & Co. Officers were offered a credit account, which could be used in any branch or when ordering by letter from anywhere in the world. They developed a range of indigo-dyed merino woollen garments in conjunction with Strachan & Co of Stroud. These clothes had a yellow selvedge with a special Gieves seal applied to the reverse side.

ENSIGN

U.S.N.

ESTIMATE

For Articles of Uniform required on Graduation.

OUTFIT LIST.

	Sterling	*Approx. Dollars*
1 Superfine Evening Dress Coat ... Stars, Gold Wire Lace, Silk Lining inclusive.	12 0 0	58-40
1 Superfine Evening Waistcoat	1 19 6	9-58
1 White Marcella Waistcoat	1 15 0	8-50
1 pair Superfine Mess Trousers, Gold Lace Stripes inclusive	7 0 0	34-02
1 Superfine Uniform Frock Coat ... Gold Wire Lace, Stars, Silk Lining inclusive.	12 0 0	58-40
1 Superfine Uniform Day Waistcoat ...	1 17 6	9-10
1 pair Superfine Uniform Trousers ...	3 16 0	18-24
1 Superfine Uniform Reefer ... ... Gold Wire Lace, Stars, inclusive	8 2 6	39-48
1 Tropical Serge Uniform Reefer ... Gold Wire Lace, Stars, inclusive.	6 12 6	32-20
1 pair Tropical Serge Trousers	2 15 0	13-36
1 Serge or Whipcord Uniform Reefer ... Gold Wire Lace, Stars, inclusive.	7 12 6	37-05
1 Serge Uniform Waistcoat	1 15 0	8-50
1 pair Serge or Whipcord Uniform Trousers	3 3 0	15-30

GIEVE'S STANDARD:

All Gold Lace and Accoutrements are guaranteed to the following assay.

Silver 90% Gold 2½% Alloy 7½%

Gieve & Co also took over the firm of Joseph Starkey Ltd, who were gold lacement and gold wire embroiderers, which meant that Gieves had control over the cap badges and gold lacing. In 1903 a shop was opened at 21 George Street in London, on the corner of Hanover Square, its main purpose being to help officers dress correctly for Court functions. The firm was soon to receive its first Royal Warrant. James Gieve also received a personal Warrant of Appointment as Royal Naval Outfitter to His Majesty King George V. The firm became Gieve, Matthers and Seagrove Ltd, but still James Gieve was very much in control of the business.

The outbreak of the First World War saw thousands of reservists being called up for military service and the demand for naval uniform stretched even Gieves' resources. The company developed an important life-saving device which took the form of an inflatable waistcoat. Flights, a Winchester based firm of military tailors, was acquired for its links with the Army. When the Royal Air Force was formed, Gieves was already involved as it had served officers in the Royal Naval Air Service.

The company went in search of new business as the demand for Navy uniforms subsided after the war, with some opportunities arising as far afield as China and Peru. New business also came from merchant ships, particularly those involved in passenger services across the Atlantic. They moved to 21 Old Bond Street and it was here that Charles Laughton came when he was cast to take the lead in *Mutiny on the Bounty*. Having made the original clothes for Captain Bligh, Gieves still had the original specifications and were able to supply authentic replicas.

James Watson Gieve was at the helm of the company for almost forty years. One day a harassed manager at the Malta branch received a visit from the chairman who showed him a letter from a midshipman serving in a battleship. The man wanted a front collar stud. Under normal circumstances, they happily would have dispatched the item by mail, but in wartime active service mail was taking weeks. Mr Gieve, always alive to the chance of good publicity, sent a representative to hand-deliver the front collar stud to a midshipman at sea – and advertise for more orders while he was there! The fleet was amused with the effrontery and kept the Malta branch busy for several months.

As with most businesses, the recession years hit Gieves but they recovered with the demand for uniforms during the Second World War. No 21 Old Bond Street was des-

FACING PAGE: *The life-saving, inflatable waistcoat, 1915*
RIGHT: *Top hats could be bought or ordered from all branches from Edinburgh to Malta*

troyed during the war and they moved to 80 Piccadilly.

In 1948, eighty-four per cent of turnover came from service requirements. However, things were changing, not least in the burgeoning demand for 'ready-to-wear' suits. Gieves felt the need to consolidate their business. A strong relationship was built up with the London and Yorkshire Trust. This proved invaluable when several members of the family died in fairly close succession. To avoid the danger of selling shares on the open market, which could have resulted in a predator company gaining an influence over the business, the Trust bought them, thereby keeping control within a small circle.

In 1974 the company acquired the well-known tailoring firm of Hawkes & Co Ltd, together with the lease of their famous premises at 1 Savile Row. 1 Savile Row was built as a private house in 1732. In 1870 it had been purchased by the Royal Geographical Society, and the Map Room of the Society was formed on the ground floor, under an extensive glass dome. It was here that the famous missionary and explorer, David Livingstone, lay in state before his burial in Westminster Abbey. Hawkes acquired the building in 1912, bringing it into commercial usage.

Hawkes & Co Ltd was founded in 1771 by Thomas Hawkes, a cap maker, garlanded with Warrants of Appointment to both His Majesty King George III and Queen Charlotte. Hawkes discovered the secret of 'jacking' leather, to make it hard enough to withstand the cut of a sword blade. Later the Duke of Wellington was to become a patron of the company.

Today Gieves & Hawkes are the acknowledged experts in all matters of correct dress. They are fully aware of the changing demands of the present-day discerning customer and have created styles to meet their needs, just as they have done for all generations. Testimony to this is the fact that in the last 100 years they have been awarded no less than seven Royal Warrants of Appointment and have made naval uniforms, using designs created in past centuries, worn by the principals and pages at the Royal Weddings of both the Prince and Princess of Wales and the Duke and Duchess of York.

The birth of the building society movement cannot be tied down to a single year with any certainty. On 3 December 1781, a society was founded in Birmingham and this date has been used for modern celebrations. This period, at the end of the eighteenth century, was a time of industrial revolution, a time when many knew poverty and deprivation. Many families moved to live in terrace houses in cities and towns which had grown rapidly as factories and mills had been built. Halifax itself has been described as a town of 'social and economic vigour', but whose 'sanitary condition was bad and whose death rate was high'. Charles Dickens described it as a 'dreadful place'.

In 1848 Halifax became a corporate borough and its first mayor was John Baldwin. Prominent men, particularly from the textile industry, had worked hard for its charter and were the same ones who worked for the formation of its building society – Colonel Akroyd, John Baldwin, Joshua Appleyard and John Abbott. A meeting was held at which the subject of establishing a permanent benefit building and investment society was discussed and its principles explained. At the first official meeting it was moved and resolved 'that a Building Society to be called the Halifax Permanent Benefit Building and Investment Society be established'. By the time the society was actually formed, however, the words 'and investment' had been dropped from the title. A secretary was appointed, Jonas Dearnley Taylor, who was to be extremely influential in directing the society's first fifty years. Subscriptions were first taken on Friday 4 February 1853. On subsequent Fridays, directors of the society were to be present punctually, fail-

LEFT: *Halifax in the high street today*
FACING PAGE, TOP: *Cover of* The Building Societies' Gazette, *1940*
FACING PAGE BELOW: *Former head offices in Halifax*

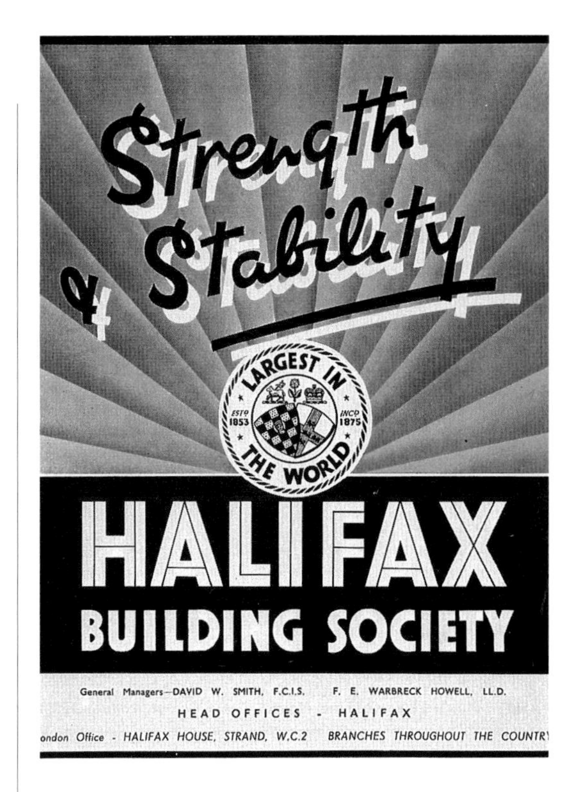

ure to do so resulting in a fine of 6d for the first hour, 1s for the second half-hour and 2s for non-attendance. Female members were fined if they failed to inform the society within two months of getting married. The rules of the society stated: 'No female shall be admitted to any office therein'!

As early as 1861 the society became involved in a scheme to provide improved housing for the working classes. Other schemes followed and so both the society and the town grew. Through such schemes working men were able to acquire, with the society's help, good houses at little more than the amount of the usual weekly rent.

While there were some difficulties in the mid-1860s, the society continued to grow and prosper. In 1871 the head-office staff had grown to six clerks and an office boy. Branches run by part-time agents operated in many West Riding towns. By 1881 its assets had passed the £1 million mark. There followed a period of stagnation, reflecting the state of the country at that time, and there was a shortage of borrowers not just at the Halifax but throughout most similar institutions. In 1891 the Liberator Building Society collapsed and this brought a lack of confidence in the Building Society Movement and a new Act in 1894. The Halifax Permanent, however, suffered little.

In 1902 Enoch Hill became secretary and almost immediately set up a new Paid Up Share Department and Penny Savings. In his first eight years, Hill doubled the society's assets. Later ideas included home

safes – small steel receptacles in which people saved coins, bringing the container every so often to the society to be emptied, counted and credited to their account. No more of these were manufactured after the Second World War, but their use continued for many years afterwards.

By 1908 the society had a larger income and was advancing more money on mortgages than any other society. In 1913 they gained the distinction of becoming the largest building society, that is in terms of total assets. This was quite an achievement to have reached in its sixtieth year.

The Halifax Equitable Building Society, an organization formed in 1871, merged with the Halifax Permanent Building Society in 1928. Even the ensuing war years failed to cause the society any real problems, although in the post-war period the Labour government's housing policy restricted private house-building in favour of the building of council houses. This meant that the lending capacity of all societies was not fully taken up. However in 1952 conditions started to improve and generally have maintained a regular demand ever since.

In 1967 the assets of the Halifax Building Society passed the £1,000 million mark, and in the next four-and-a-half years doubled again. In 1995 the Halifax Building Society and the Leeds Permanent Building Society agreed to merge. The new society, which retains the name of the Halifax Building Society, has assets of £93,000 million and will have almost 2.5 million mortgagees. The number of branches is now over 1,100 with staff totalling some 28,000. It is of course the largest building society in the United Kingdom and probably the largest housing finance institution in the world.

ABOVE AND BELOW: *Advertisements from 1930*

The history of the Hamley family in Cornwall probably goes back beyond the time of the Norman Conquest. The spelling has varied, the form 'Hamlyn' being found in the Domesday Book of 1087. It is almost certain that the 'toyshop' family originated in Cornwall.

Directories for the Holborn area in the early 1800s show several members of the Hamley family engaged in shop businesses, particularly as watch and clock makers and as tobacconists. In 1800, 231 High Holborn is shown as a 'Toy Warehouse' (ie shop) owned by Ben Pearsall. By 1811 an entry lists William Hamley, a timber merchant, and so it may have been that Hamley worked with Pearsall, perhaps supplying wood for the construction of the toys for which Hamleys were famous from the earliest days.

A second William Hamley, born in 1803, second son of John Hamley, a carpenter, took over the Toy Warehouse in 1830. It became known as 'Noah's Ark', a name it kept for many years, the Noah's Ark being one of the main toys it sold, a toy based on the Bible story and therefore one which could be played with on a Sunday. The shop had for many years a Noah's Ark symbol over the door.

Hamley aimed to sell the very best, and other toys included tin soldiers, rag dolls, hoops and wooden hobby horses. This William Hamley married twice, marrying two sisters and had four sons and two

TOP: *Advertisement from* Festival of Britain Guide
RIGHT: *200 Regent Street, London*

daughters. By 1861 his eldest son William Henry was helping him in the shop and it was about this time they acquired the celebrated conjuring and magical business, Blands of 35 New Oxford Street. So well known were they that a letter addressed to 'Hamley's Magical Palace, Europe' reached its destination.

When William Hamley died in 1874, he left strict instructions in his will for his business to be continued by two of his sons, William Henry and Francis James (known as Frank). By 1875 they had opened another branch at 12 Oxford Street, and later on at 64 Regent Street. Although both sons had descendants, the business was eventually continued by their brother Edwin, contrary to their father's instructions.

A personal glimpse in a family letter describes William Henry Hamley as he rode daily on a bus to Holborn: 'I can see now Mr Wm Hamley, always a flower in his coat. A florist in the Seven Sisters Road used to have one ready for him every morning.' The writer also describes a toy of the period called 'The Walking Postman': 'A postman pushing a parcel-post barrow. You held one wheel, with the other you wound up a piece of elastic and then put it on the ground. Result – in the unwinding of the elastic the truck moved along.'

The range of toys increased to include dolls, games, wooden puzzles and sports equipment, some imported from Europe, Japan and America. They always took a pride in the quality of their toys and when, in 1901, *The Times* published a letter complaining about dirty stuffing in a toy, Hamleys stated that *their* stuffed toys contained only clean stuffing, even challenging the complainant to cut open any of their toys to check the fact.

Edwin Hamley eventually married Ada Mellicent Dege, whose sister Florence ran a factory for disabled men who made Noah's Arks for Hamleys.

Hamleys stores have suffered several times from fire and a letter from the period reminds us of life a century ago: 'Up dashed a hansom cab and in it a porter from Holborn. No telephone in those days you know. [The porter] Rushed into the garden and

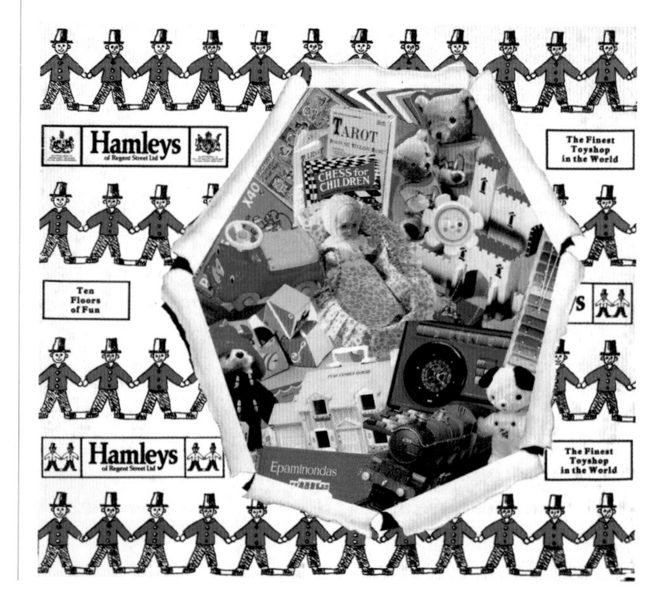

FACING PAGE, TOP: *William Hamley II*
FACING PAGE, BOTTOM: *1975 catalogue showing men designed by Peggy Lines*
RIGHT: *Ping Pong set*

shouted out "Come on, sir, all the shop's on fire" . . . Off dashed your uncle and Mr Binko in the waiting cab . . . It [the fire] was luckily stopped in the basement and after it there was a marvellous sale of salvaged toys.'

In 1901 a new game called Gossima was introduced and launched exclusively through Hamleys. It was an immediate success, the public calling it Ping Pong, an onomatopoeic name. By 1921 it had officially become known as Table Tennis.

After the original Noah's Ark premises were burnt down, an ambitious building scheme was put in hand and in 1921 a fine six-storey building was completed at 200–2 Regent Street, but due to the expense involved and the Depression, Hamleys were forced into liquidation in 1931.

G & J Lines had started supplying Hamleys with rocking horses and other wooden toys towards the end of the nineteenth century. Walter, the son of Joseph Lines, had as a boy sat on a horse-drawn van when it was making deliveries to Hamleys. The two families knew each other and Walter had developed a great love for the store. Lines Brothers, founded in 1919, had become famous for their Triang Toys, and Walter, by then chairman, is quoted as saying: 'I always wanted a toy shop, so I decided to get the best in the world.' He raised a bank loan on his own security and purchased Hamleys; he then distributed fifty-eight per cent of the shares to Lines Bros, the rest to family and friends.

Walter Lines's existing Queen Mary's Royal Warrant, as supplier to the Royal Household, and for achievement to export was transferred to him as chairman of Hamleys, at his own request. This was later followed by Queen Elizabeth II's Warrant. Both are prominently displayed above the main store's entrance.

The Hamley family link was continued by Edwin's son, Cedric Hamley, who had worked at the Regent Street store as a young man. In 1929 he opened a store at Croydon, trading there as C Hamley, and when he retired it was sold back to the Regent Street company.

During the Second World War the Regent Street store was damaged on no less than five occasions, but although only two floors remained open, the store never closed. Staff wearing tin hats served at the front door, rushing in to collect the required toys, and then handing them over to the customer at the same door.

After the war, business once again expanded and at the 1951 Festival of Britain

Exhibition, Hamleys provided a grand dolls' salon and a magnificent model railway layout. Walter Lines was chairman for many years and during that time sixteen buyers scoured the world's toy fairs for new toys to bring back to the store. When he retired in the 1960s he was succeeded by his daughter H K P (Peggy) Lines.

Peggy Lines is particularly remembered as the one who designed the famous little men on Hamleys' bags. One evening in about 1965 she took home a pile of typing paper and pots of red and black ink and sat into the small hours scribbling away. She wanted a design that would have real impact, but not use a specific toy – she always considered Hamleys much more than just a toy shop. Next morning she presented Mr Reynolds, the general manager with six designs. He said 'That one' and today they are seen throughout the world as tourists take home treasured presents in the famous bags.

In 1976 Hamleys passed into the hands of Debenhams. It was soon after this that the company moved to 188–96 Regent Street, the premises they occupy today. Over the next few years the company changed hands several times before Howard Dyer and Stephen Woodbridge were appointed to take over the management of the company in 1991. In 1994 it was floated on the Stock Market and became a public company. Other, smaller shops have also been opened at Gatwick and Heathrow airports and in Covent Garden.

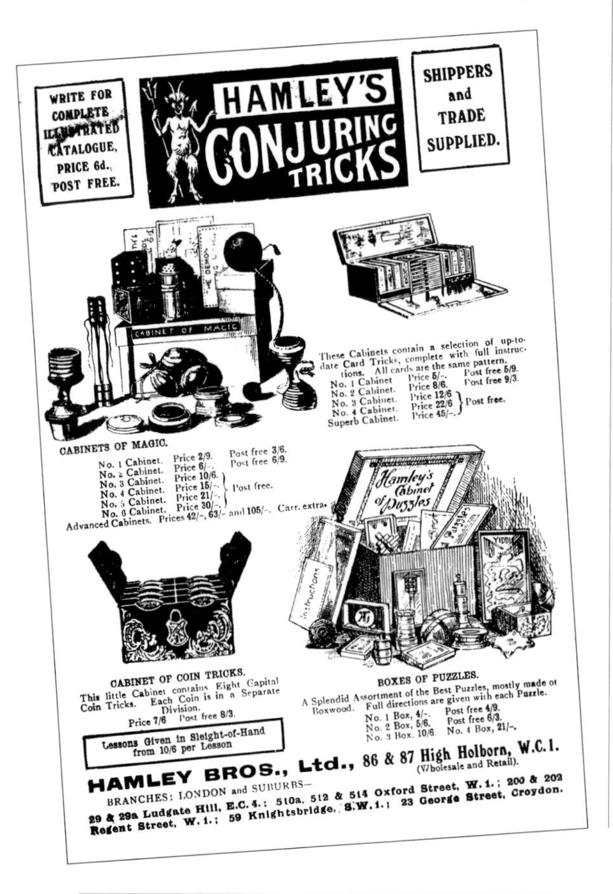

ABOVE AND LEFT: *Advertisements showing diversity of merchandise*

Harrods KNIGHTSBRIDGE

Charles Henry Harrod was born in 1799 in Lexdon in Essex and became a miller at Clacton in Essex. In 1834 he moved to London and began selling tea and other groceries, developing both a wholesale and retail trade in the Stepney area. He had married Elizabeth Digby, the daughter of a pork butcher, in 1830 and of their five children, two of whom died in infancy, it is Charles Digby, born in 1841 who became a grocer.

During the 1840s Charles Henry took over a small grocery shop in Knightsbridge from a wholesaler friend, Philip Henry Burden, moving into the house behind the shop at 8 Middle Queen's Building, part of what is now Brompton Road. The shop had a turnover of about £20 per week.

In 1851 the Great Exhibition took place in Hyde Park and, as a result, Knightsbridge became transformed from a poor slum area into one of London's fashionable areas, especially as new buildings were erected along the Cromwell Road and in South Kensington.

Charles Digby learnt his trade as a grocer, serving an apprenticeship with another business before coming to work for his father. In 1860 his mother died, and Harrod Snr, now already sixty, decided to hand the business over to his son. He did not, however, give it to his son, but sold it to him for a reported sum of £500.

In 1864 Charles paid his father the last instalment and put his own nameplate in the window. That same year he married Caroline Godsmark. He soon made his mark by banning credit and by cutting his prices. At that time many firms allowed generous credit which servants took advantage of, but which led to bad practices and increased costs. Putting an end to such established ways was a risk, but he managed to hold on to his customers and hence prospered.

Three years later a new shop front, complete with a plate glass window, was put in place and the range of items on sale was extended to include patent medicines, perfume and stationery. By 1868 the turnover had risen to £1000 per week and he was employing sixteen staff.

As the years progressed so the firm prospered. The family moved from the shop firstly to Esher and later to Sydenham, from where Harrod travelled daily by pony and trap. In June 1870 he introduced a sixty-five-page catalogue listing the many items he had on offer, but still reminding potential customers that the prices were for cash. Delivery services were available to any part of the country. People were reminded that 'Mr Harrod begs to mention that he sells EXCLUSIVELY FOR CASH. All country orders MUST BE PAID FOR previous to them being dispatched.'

PREVIOUS PAGE: *Charles Henry Harrod*
LEFT: *Food Hall*
FACING PAGE, TOP: *Father Christmas delivery van*
FACING PAGE, BOTTOM: *Harrods at night*

In 1874 the name Harrod's Store appeared on the windows for the first time, encouraging ladies and gentlemen to come in their carriages to the store. For his most important customers he would personally show them selected items of stock. As more room became available so a major rebuilding programme was embarked upon, to be completed in time for the Christmas trade of 1883. A massive fire broke out late on 6 December which destroyed the building, complete with Christmas stock. The next day, a letter went out to their customers saying: 'I greatly regret to inform you that in consequence of the above premises being burnt down, your order will be delayed in the execution a day or two. I hope, in the course of Tuesday or Wednesday next, to be able to forward it. In the meantime, may I ask your indulgence.' Temporary premises were opened in Humphrey's Hall in Knightsbridge and were filled with new stock by the following Monday. That year's Christmas trade beat all his previous records.

The disaster gave Harrod the opportunity to design and rebuild a new store which could incorporate his many ideas. By September 1884 the store was ready for opening, and the sympathy of press and public ensured that sales would grow at significant speed. In 1880 he had introduced his 'own brand' groceries, wrapped in a patriotic red, white and blue. New departments were also introduced, which included Poultry, Wines and Spirits, Jewellery and China and Glass. Cash desks replaced messenger boys who had previously brought customers their change. He was also persuaded to break his 'no credit' rule, and among early creditworthy people were Oscar Wilde, Lillie Langtry and Ellen Terry.

The new store had five floors, although only two of them were sales floors, joined by a grand central staircase. Even so, within two years, a further extension was added. By now, however, the strain of the years was taking a toll on Harrod's health and he finally retired in 1889. The business became a limited liability company and Harrod was paid out in cash for £120,000. Charles Digby Harrod went to live in Somerset and later moved to Sussex.

Now the store was under the control of a general manager, William Smart, but soon signs of decline were obvious. Through an intermediary, Edgar Cohen, whom Harrod had made a friend of and who had advised him on financial affairs, Harrod was persuaded to return. He was appalled at what he saw and did what he could to improve things while seeking for a more suitable replacement.

The man he found was Richard Burbridge, who was in his mid-forties and who had good experience in other leading stores of the period. He was to be the architect for the future development of the company.

In 1894 he was initiating further expansion and over the next few years he was adding a new redeveloped block each summer, one of them being completed in less than six weeks. Burbridge had the vision of the store owning the whole island site and when they had acquired the whole of the frontage to Brompton Road the now famous terracotta façade, fired by Royal Doulton, was commenced. By 1908 staff numbers had risen to 4,000.

New initiatives took place, such as in 1898 when they unveiled London's first escalator. The sale of motor cars started in 1902.

In 1911 Burbridge's dream came true, the whole four-and-a-half-acre island site was finally Harrods. The Queen of Norway granted them their first Royal Warrant, followed by Queen Mary in 1913. Today they hold four Royal Warrants. Shops such as Dickins & Jones, D H Evans, Kendal Milne and Swan & Edgar were gradually acquired.

Richard Burbridge's son and later his grandson ran the company until the House of Fraser takeover in 1959. While the Lonrho Group tried to gain control of the House of Fraser Group, and thereby Harrods, this was not to be and in 1985 the Alfayed Investment and Trust (UK) PLC paid £615 million for the remaining equity of the group. In 1986 Mohamed Al Fayed became Chairman of Harrods and has continued to play a positive role in the store's development, especially as it is once again a private company.

The largest store in Europe, Harrods employs 3,500 staff, with daily takings in the region of £1.5 million. Small branches have also opened at airports in Frankfurt, Vienna, Hamburg and Terminals 3 and 4 at Heathrow. They have a presence in Japan and a further outlet on board *Queen Elizabeth II*.

Our Harry Ramsden, the famous Harry Ramsden, was the son of Harry Ramsden who was also a fish-and-chip man. A bit of a 'rough diamond', Harry Ramsden Snr opened a fish-and-chip shop at 22 Manchester Road, Bradford, around the turn of the century in a very humble, working-class district. His children were expected to help in the shop, be it chopping potatoes, filleting fish, lighting the coal fire, frying or serving.

Harry Ramsden Jnr had a mind of his own. While he was still attending school part-time, he also worked at Ambler's mill, leaving home at 4am to start work at 5am, and at a barber's, later progressing to become a telegram delivery boy. After some years in the taxicab business, he decided to become a publican. The Craven Heifer had been allowed to become run down and had virtually no regular customers, but Harry soon noticed that the neighbouring pub was doing a good trade. The secret to his rival's success was that he had a pianist. Harry paid the pianist double to swap his allegiances! However, the magistrates would not grant him a music licence so Harry posted look-outs to warn of a likely visit from the law.

After the First World War, Harry did not return to the licensed trade but instead set up his first fish-and-chip shop in a lock-up at Wibsey Fair, about two miles from the centre of Bradford. Thanks to his wife, Beatrice, providing theatrical artists with digs, comedians' thanks came as free advertising as they worked into their patter the fact that they had been to Harry Ramsden's for fish and chips! He then opened a shop in Manchester Road at the junction with Bower Street. At this shop, he opened from lunch through to the evening, every day of the year. When questioned about opening at Christmas, he replied, 'Especially at Christmas, don't you get bloody fed up of turkey?'

Following on from his success, he opened a further shop in Westgate, bought the clothing shop next door and turned it into the Cosy Cafe. He decorated it with the black and white tiles and hunting prints, which were to become his trademark in years to come. By this time, Beatrice had contracted tuberculosis and their son Harry was also a frail and sickly lad. They needed to be in a place where the air was clean and fresh and so, in 1928, Harry bought a lock-up fish-and-chip shop in Otley Road, White Cross, for £150. They lived in a cottage across the road, but sadly, in 1929, Beatrice died, never to see the glory that was to come.

These were the years of the Depression and of great poverty in the working-class districts of northern industrial towns and cities. By Friday little would be left, either in food or in money, and at that time the fish-and-chip shop provided a cheap meal. As a result there were fish-and-chip shops on many street corners, where fish cost 2d and chips a penny.

Harry was most precise in many things – not least in the temperature of the hot fat in the frying range. 'There was no chip ever cut by man which could not be cooked to perfection in three minutes,' he would say.

He had thermometers cut into the frying pans, knew exactly how deep the fat should be and of course the batter recipe was a secret. He had a list of 100 items of hygiene and orderliness to be ticked off before he ever left the shop. He encouraged his staff to improve efficiency and offered £1 reward for practical ideas.

The restaurant which seated 200 was far ahead of its time. It had wall-to-wall carpeting, chandeliers and leaded lights at the windows, which provoked one lad to ask his father, 'Is this where God comes for his fish

FACING PAGE, TOP: *1952, celebrating twenty-one years in business*
FACING PAGE, BOTTOM: *Staff on parade with Harry seated at front*
TOP: *Crowds queuing for fish and chips*
RIGHT: *White Cross restaurant, 1936*
OVERLEAF: *Harry Ramsden's as it is today*

and chips?' On a raised area at the far end of the restaurant the pianist, often Harry Corbett, Harry Ramsden's cousin, would play for the customers' enjoyment. Harry Corbett was later to become famous with his bear glove-puppet, Sooty. Out of the restaurant, but to him a most important part of the facilities, the toilets were spotless, with soap in the washroom changed three or four times a day. Harry looked after the 'take-away' customers as well, providing a covered area with seats and some tables each with salt and vinegar, and later a cup of tea.

As the years of the motor car materialized so it became increasingly obvious that Harry had chosen a splendid site. It was on the main route from Bradford and Leeds to the west coast resorts of Blackpool and Morecambe, for the Yorkshire Dales and for the Lake District. They were also at the heart of local industry and therefore he lost no opportunity offering local firms such as Crompton Parkinson and Silver Cross prams a delivery service of fish and chips.

Harry did not take on any grand manner with his success. He was happiest when he was in his small caravan. On 7 July 1952, Harry celebrated twenty-one years of business on the White Cross site, and he made it a day to remember for thousands of people. (I was there!) He sold fish at a penny and chips at a halfpenny, the same price his father had charged all those days long ago before the First World War.

In 1954 Harry brought in Eddie Stokes as manager, giving him an option to buy the business, although he stayed on as a director of the new company until his death in 1963. Eddie Stokes later sold the business to Associated Fisheries who, in 1988, sold it to Merryweathers. Today it is a public company with branches at Heathrow Airport, Blackpool, Manchester, Cardiff, and now in Hong Kong and with plans for Melbourne. For many years people from many parts of the world have known of Harry Ramsden's fish and chips. It is the aim to provide that same quality wherever the name of Harry Ramsden is placed above a fish-and-chip restaurant.

John Hatchard was born on 17 October 1768. After a brief apprenticeship to a master printer, in June 1782 Hatchard went to work for a bookseller and publisher by the name of Ginger whose shop was in Great College Street in Westminster.

During the next seven years he must have come into contact with many well-known literary people, even if he was only a messenger boy. Perhaps it was meeting such people or perhaps it was the books he saw in the shop that awakened in him the ambition to own a bookshop of his own. In those days many of them had a 'back parlour', into which authors and the better clients would be invited for conversation or a smoke and a drink, something he would want to have in his establishment.

At the end of his apprenticeship, Hatchard became a shopman with Mr Thomas Payne, a noted bookseller, and on 30 June 1797, at the age of twenty-nine, John Hatchard left the shop and started working for himself. While Regent Street had not been built at this stage, Piccadilly was already a busy highway and close by were the areas of the aristocracy, the Haymarket, St James's Street and Pall Mall. There were several bookshops along Piccadilly already, including Debrett's, but Hatchard felt there was room for one more and that he could attract some members of the aristocracy to his premises.

On 1 July 1797 he took over 173 Piccadilly for which he had to pay £31 10*s*. for the goodwill and £40 per annum rent. He was fortunate that Mr Payne was not jealous of his enterprize but, rather, encouraged Hatchard in all that he did, not even taking exception when some of his clients moved to the new shop.

John Hatchard was one of a growing number of Evangelical Christians. He was also a Tory, opposed to infidelity and strict about his faith and morals. Soon after starting his business he published a pamphlet entitled *Reform or Ruin: Take Your Choice* by John Bowdler, which was an immediate success and the foundation of his fortunes. Soon afterwards he was appointed publisher to *The Christian Observer* and also for the *Reports of the Society for Bettering the Condition of the Poor*. In later years the Society, which included such famous names as

PREVIOUS PAGE: *Watercolour of Hatchards today by Francis Katz*
LEFT: *Hatchards in the 1820s with window display of opened books*
FACING PAGE: *Advertisement from 1955*

William Wilberforce, Sir Thomas Bernard, and Pitt's brother-in-law, E J Eliot, met at Hatchards, regarding it as a club. This organization had as one of its main objectives the Abolition of the Slave Trade. Another great organization also saw its birth at Hatchards, for on 7 March 1804 a meeting was held for 'the purpose of instituting a Society for the Improvement of Horticulture', the Horticultural Society, later the Royal Horticultural Society.

In the summer of 1801, Hatchard moved to larger premises at 190 Piccadilly, purchasing a twenty-four-year lease for 1,000 guineas, 500 guineas to be paid at the time, the remainder within two years. Only four years earlier he had been worth only £5! Clearly he was now one of London's leading booksellers. Disraeli wrote: 'Debrett's was the chief haunt of the Whigs; Hatchards, I believe, of the Tories. It was at the latter house that my father, Isaac d'Israeli, made the acquaintance of Mr Pye' (Poet Laureate).

In 1814 Hatchard published a catalogue of available books which ran to some 7,000 items, and sold for three shillings. A few years later the business moved again, this time to 187 Piccadilly. His famous customers included Lord Grosvenor, Wellington, Lord Derby, W E Gladstone, Robert Peel and Palmerston. The Hatchard family lived over the shop for many years but later had a house in semi-rural Clapham.

John Hatchard died on 21 June 1849, in his eighty-first year, by which time his children were themselves middle-aged. It was the second son, Thomas Hatchard, who carried on the business. Thomas was not of the same stature as his father and ran the company for rather less than ten years, dying in 1858. With no male Hatchard to carry on the business, Henry Hudson, a great-grandson of the founder, successfully carried the business through to 1880. As the century progressed the company relinquished its publishing activities, but continued to flourish as a bookseller.

In 1881 Hatchards advertised for a junior assistant, who was 'a good writer, quick, active, industrious, and thoroughly steady and respectable, with some knowledge of the retail trade'. Arthur L Humphreys, who had a couple of years' experience with the old-fashioned bookseller, William Mack, stayed with the firm for the next half-century, much of that time as the leading figure in the business.

It is from Humphreys that we get a clear picture of the situation in the 1880s: 'The building at 187 Piccadilly, where the business was conducted, was then one of the old residential houses, and in former days the

Hatchard Family lived in a large part of the front upper floors. At the back and on the lower floors there were heaps of narrow staircases, dark corners and low-ceilinged attics all fitted with books. An atmosphere rather sombre and religious hung over the whole place. The assistants seemed to me to be all very old men either with beards or with side whiskers . . . Here in Piccadilly I saw the best of everything.' Fine carriages would roll up to the black and gold pillars, where great men like Lord Shaftesbury would alight. There were still some who were accompanied by powdered footmen in breeches and white stockings.

Humphreys had always adored books, he had a good memory for faces and customers began to take an interest in the young assistant who remembered their wants and was always cheerful and helpful. As the clientele took notice, so did the management and he advanced within the company.

One day Lady Warwick came into Hatchards and asked Humphreys to find a copy of a particular sermon by Bishop Ken. He suddenly remembered that he had seen a lot of seventeenth-century sermons bound together in another bookshop. He rushed round and persuaded them to split up the volume, and the following day Lady Warwick got her sermon! Obviously she was much impressed, and she asked that he be allowed to help her build up her private library. Such tasks were soon to become an important part of the business and this involved the young man travelling up and down the country buying and selling collections.

In March 1891, a former apprentice, Edwin A M Shepherd, bought Hatchards and took into partnership A L Humphreys. Although the publishing arm had been sold off, Humphreys went ahead and reprinted some of the old classics on handmade paper, calling the series 'The Royal Library'. On the third floor a much-enlarged 'secondhand' department was housed, and the work of developing private libraries was enhanced with a commission to be responsible for the private library of the Prince of Wales at Sandringham.

HATCHARDS

Booksellers to Their Majesties The King, The Queen, and to Queen Mary

offer Country book-lovers a magnificent range of informative and fascinating reading matter . . . new and second-hand.

Visit this famous old Bookshop next time you are in London, or write your requirements to:

187 PICCADILLY, W.1

(*REGent* 3201–4)

In the Spring of 1893 Cecil Rhodes was brought into the shop by a friend and from this meeting arose a lifetime's work of translating and printing documents from other languages. The glorious years of the 1890s saw more famous clients at Hatchards, including Rudyard Kipling and G K Chesterton. The name of Hatchards has remained prominent this century, although it has undergone several changes of ownership. A L Humphreys severed his connection with the firm in 1924, but Edwin Shepherd's sons were to continue into the Second World War.

The immediate post-war years were difficult for Hatchards but in 1960 it was taken over by the publisher Sir William Collins and subsequently enjoyed a successful period. It was during this time that Tommy Joy LVO was managing director at Collins and came to be regarded as the doyen of booksellers. Following the death of Sir William Collins shares were sold to Rupert Murdoch, but in 1990 Pentos took over what is still one of the best-known names in bookselling. When Pentos collapsed in 1995 Hatchards came into the ownership of Thorn EMI.

HEAL'S

Ambrose and Rachel Heal lived at Milton on Stour, Gillingham in Dorset. They had two sons, John Harris Heal and Ambrose Heal, whose future they did not see in the West Country but in the new commercial life of the capital.

It was at the turn of the nineteenth century that they separately entered the bedding business in London. Ambrose's wife's family owned a linen factory and a bed ticking warehouse, while John Harris started as a feather-dresser with a firm in Leicester Square which dealt in real ostrich feathers, and subsequently started his own feather-dressing business in 1810 at 33 Rathbone Place. About the same time, he married Fanny Brewer and the following year they had their first child John Harris.

In 1818 Heal moved his business to 203 Tottenham Court Road, a developing area which was to become known as the 'Furnishing Street of London'. At that time bedding would often be a simple straw palliasse topped with a simple hair or wool mattress. Only those who had more money could afford a feather mattress.

When in 1833 John Harris Heal died, the business was carried on by his wife who renamed it Fanny Heal & Son, Bedding Manufacturers. In 1840 they bought up Miller's Stables and Capper's Farm, where John Harris Jnr and his wife lived and they moved the firm to 196 Tottenham Court Road.

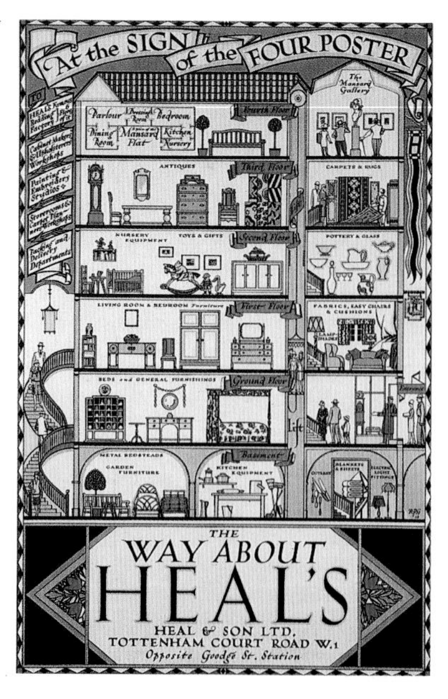

Fanny and John Harris Heal were to lay the foundations of a bedmaking business which was far ahead of its competitors, for not only had they a feather-dressing mill and wool-carding machine, but four years later they added a steam plant for purifying and dressing the feathers.

In 1846 the firm became known as John Harris Heal & Son, before being shortened the following year to Heal & Son. While John Harris had taken control in 1840, he had realized long before that the works of Charles Dickens, produced in monthly instalments, were ideal places to advertise, and, starting with *The Pickwick Papers*, this was to continue for the next twenty-eight years. The Heals had a consuming interest in advertising and were to exploit its benefits over many years.

As the railways developed, so he advertised on railway station platforms, encouraging travellers to visit the premises in Tottenham Court Road, and announcing his latest innovation, his catalogue. This was really a mail order price list; due to improved rail and Post Office services, it was now possible for Heal's to supply a much wider area. Year by year the range of furnishings offered grew, and in the 1852 catalogue they illustrated no fewer than sixty-seven patterns of iron and brass bedsteads and cribs (these were fashionable as it was said that bed bugs and lice could not scale the slippery legs). The catalogue also contained a wide range of mahogany four-poster and half-tester bedsteads.

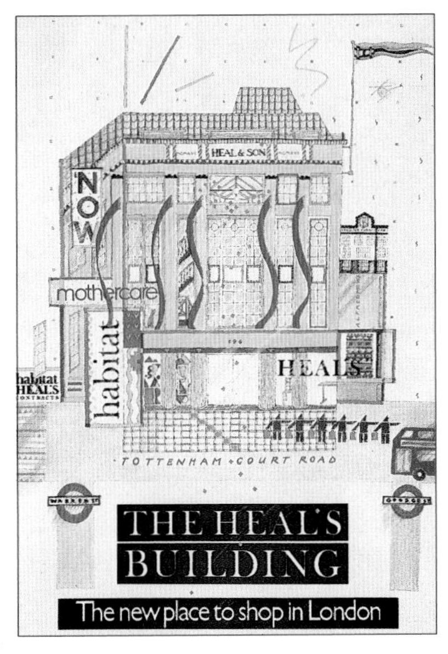

Mattress development was continually taking place and their best mattress is likely to have been the French Mattress, a luxurious sandwich of long East India wool around a filling of the best black horse hair. Spring mattresses were also introduced to replace the palliasse, but they were expensive and cumbersome; John developed a hinged one made in three sections lashed together, which he patented in 1860 under the name Sommier Elastique Portatif, the French name giving it special cachet. During the 1860s they began to export goods to meet the growing needs of people in the Colonies, but the export catalogue was not a success.

Another innovation was soon to follow where potential customers were invited to see a series of small rooms in which bedroom suites would be set out to show how they would look in the customer's home.

John Harris Heal ran the business for thirty-six years, a period of great development and success. While many firms stocked machine-made furniture, particularly for the new rich, Heal's retained their own cabinet-making factory, where excellence of craftsmanship was of paramount importance, and where future generations of the business were taught. Ambrose Heal Jnr, John Harris's son, was one of these.

Ambrose Heal was a sensitive furniture designer as well as an excellent shopkeeper. He gained experience at the bench in some of the specialist workplaces of the day before joining Heal's in 1893; the first catalogue of his work appeared in 1895, and founded the Heal's style. His limited edition desks, tables and chests of drawers are still regarded as design classics. Even his catalogue was looked upon as a book to treasure and keep as a work of reference.

Ambrose Heal became a member of the Arts and Crafts Exhibition Society and exhibited for the first time in 1899. His works were of fumed oak with steel handles and hinges. As a result of his work being seen in the exhibition he received a commission from the Hotel Standard at Norrkoping in Sweden to design and supply all its furniture and furnishings, and so started a relationship with Scandinavia that was to become most important. Bedroom furniture for the Paris Exhibition of 1900 featured façades framed in a distinctive chequer-board design which was later to become a trade mark of all Heal's graphic design. The *Architectural Review* described their furniture as a 'triumph of craftsmanship'.

Ambrose Heal introduced the four-poster trademark in 1904, but over the years its design was modified. He reached out to customers in the new London suburbs of Richmond, Barnes, Clapham and Kentish Town, as well as the new garden cities of Hampstead, Letchworth and Welwyn. While they continued to sell the higher-priced, hand-crafted pieces, they began to sell cheaper, machine-made items, but still with the same high quality of design. These latter items were sought after by the new middle class. They also sold painted furniture

which was described in the catalogues as being 'excellent for servants' bedrooms'.

In 1907 Heal & Son was converted from a partnership into a limited company, with Ambrose Heal as managing director; he later became chairman on the death of his father in 1913. That same year, Ambrose Heal's cousin, Cecil Brewer, was given the task of working on a new building at 195–196 Tottenham Court Road, which was later to be hailed as a landmark in shop architecture. The building had five floors, each with its own speciality. On the top floor, the Mansard Gallery, lit by dormers behind a parapet, led out into a winter garden, which then led into a small open-court area, paved in red tiles and with a fountain. This was all designed to give a countrified atmosphere and complement the room sets in the gallery. Brewer also designed a new bedding factory, which provided innovations like dust extractors, air conditioning, fire escapes and a sprinkler system.

In 1915, Ambrose Heal was a founder of the Design and Industries Association, a forerunner of the Design Council, which linked design and industry.

After the First World War fewer people had servants, so the emphasis had to change towards providing furniture with easy-to-clean finishes. Heal's used a secret recipe to produce 'weathered oak'. In 1927 they gained their first Royal Appointment from George V. The King already had a wireless cabinet, which had been designed by Ambrose and presented to him in 1924 by the BBC in an effort to stimulate his interest in broadcasting.

To encourage the development of an interest in contemporary design Heal's started producing their Signed Edition Series, which were not only beautiful but particularly practical.

The 1920s and 30s with their economic uncertainty brought a decline to the bedding department, but this was countered by

SPRING MATTRESSES.

SOMMIER ELASTIQUE PORTATIF (HEAL & SON'S Patent), made in three parts, is still the most comfortable Spring Mattress yet invented, and with a Best French or Best Hair Top Mattress makes a very superior bed.

No. 4. BEST STUFFED SPRING MATTRESS, stuffed throughout with Best Horsehair; also made to fold in half.
BEST GERMAN SPRING MATTRESS, similar to above but made with soft elastic sides. The softest and most luxurious spring made.

PREVIOUS PAGES: *Posters from 1928 (left) and 1984 (right)*
ABOVE: *121 years' business*
LEFT: *Spring mattress, devised by John Heal and patented in 1860*
FACING PAGE: *Ambrose Heal's earliest sets of bedroom furniture – the Newlyn suite*

the introduction of chromium-plated tubular furniture. In 1931 the outlook for the company was very bad and it was announced that unless the staff took a ten per cent pay cut, and the directors a larger one, then the company would not be able to carry on. Heal's had to sell lower-priced furniture, and this was made for them by Greenings of Oxford. These actions pulled them back from the brink.

Ambrose Heal realized that the public must be made aware of these new developments and launched an enormous promotional campaign which included an illustrated booklet being sent to 38,000 potential customers who lived in houses or flats with a rental value of more than £50, and had a telephone. Among all the gloom came recognition of the service Ambrose Heal had contributed, not just to Heal's, but to the whole area of furniture design, when he was knighted.

After the depression, when business was more buoyant, the shop was extended to include 197–199 Tottenham Court Road. It was designed by Sir Edward Maufe, the architect of Guildford Cathedral.

During the Second World War, in a six-month period, Heal's made for the Admiralty 77,000 hair beds and 19,000 pillows before later moving into the manufacture of large numbers of parachutes. After the war Anthony Heal became chairman and Christopher Heal became design director. Again it was a time of change, with the introduction of new manufacturing techniques and very different styles. One example of this was Plymet furniture made of aluminium sheet veneered with figured ash or rosewood. The metal-cored plywood was curved to form the outside skin of the furniture and was bonded to a structural frame of steel.

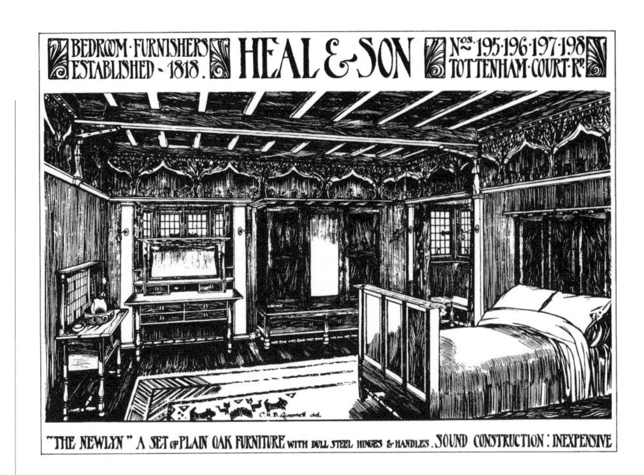

The 1950s and 60s were good years for Heal's and it was during this period that Sir Ambrose received the Royal Society of Arts Albert Gold Medal for services to industrial design. When he died in 1959 it was said of him that he had 'the eye of an eagle, an integrity of design and of shopkeeping, and that his taste was unquestionable'.

As the company approached its 150th anniversary it was awarded Queen Elizabeth II's Royal Warrant. In only six years Heal's turnover had doubled to exceed £2 million and in 1965 it was awarded the Royal Society of Arts' first Presidential Medal for Design Management. The 1970s were difficult trading times and in 1983 the company was sold to Sir Terence Conran. It was the end of an era, particularly for the Heal family.

Terence Conran, founder of Habitat, now bought all the Heal family shares for around £4.8 million. An excellent designer, he upgraded the stores, redrew the four-poster logo and Ambrose Heal's design for bed ticking was used for some of the packaging. Throughout all these changes the Heal's staff remained enthusiastic and gave the proposals their support. In 1990 Heal's had a management buy-out and is now a small independent company with the original store in Tottenham Court Road, another in the King's Road, which opened in December 1995, and a smaller store in Guildford.

JAEGER

Gustav Jaeger was born in Wurtemberg in Germany in 1832. He studied zoology in Stuttgart and medicine in Tubingen; being a Protestant, however, he was debarred from accepting the chair of zoology at Vienna. In 1866 he returned to Stuttgart where he was appointed lecturer to the Agricultural Academy, the Royal Polytechnic School and the Veterinary College. He was one of the first scientists on the Continent to adopt Darwinian theories, supporting them with his own original research which was recognized by Darwin in his letters.

Jaeger became particularly interested in the spirit and the soul, and in astronomy. He also believed that the elimination of water from tissues was conducive to good health and a protection against disease. From these principles came his system of clothing the body, day and night, in porous, pure wool, thus maintaining an equable temperature of the skin and allowing free evaporation of the moisture thrown off.

TOP: *Gustav Jaeger*
LEFT: *Ladies' wear*
OVERLEAF: *Boys' suits*

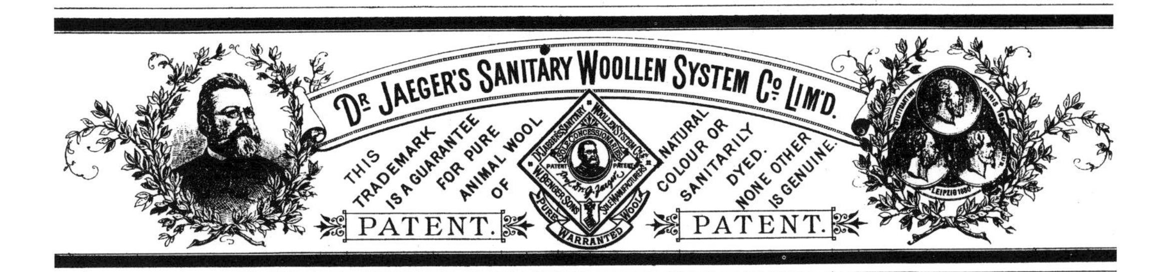

In 1880, Lewis Tomalin read Jaeger's book on health culture, advocating that people should dress in clothes made entirely of animal hair – principally wool – and avoid vegetable fibres like cotton and linen. In February 1884 Tomalin opened the first Jaeger shop in Fore Street in the City of London, not as a commercial venture, but as a gesture of philanthropy. Tomalin was so convinced by Jaeger's arguments that he burned all the family linen and replaced it with items made of fine woollen taffeta. Tomalin obtained a licence from Dr Jaeger to use his name and imported merchandise from Germany made in accordance with his theory. Over the door he put the sign: Dr Jaeger's Sanitary Woollen System.

With Jaeger being awarded a gold medal at a London health exhibition and prominent members of society promoting the clothes, Tomalin's enterprize was a great success. Oscar Wilde had sponsored an article which appeared in *The Times*, George Bernard Shaw created a sensation by walking around London wearing a brown knitted Jaeger suit, looking like a brown gnome, and Ambrose Heal made woollen mattresses to sell in his famous furniture shop.

More shops were opened and items for sale were now manufactured in England, including five-toed socks (which had to be made by a glove manufacturer), all designed for health culture. Tomalin refused to employ anyone who had previous experience of the clothing trade for fear that they might try to adulterate the message.

Jaeger clothing was taken to many parts of the globe: Stanley took it to Africa when he went looking for Dr Livingstone, Nansen took it on his first great Polar expedition, Scott on his journey to the Arctic – and of course these all helped to make the business prosper. By 1900 there were twenty shops and a wholesale company supplying agents in many parts of the country. It was around this time that Jaeger first introduced camel hair from the Asian two-humped camel.

When Lewis Tomalin's son, H F Tomalin, came into the business he sought to widen the range of stock by printing art nouveau designs on wool fibres. Jaeger coats, for men and women, although of classic style, became very popular and pointed the way to the future development of the company.

During the First World War, they concentrated on making sleeping bags, woollens and underwear. After the war, the 'hygiene' sales angle had lost its appeal. The transition from shops selling a 'sanitary woollen system' to leading fashion house was not easy. They had the beautiful fabrics but the styles were 'awful', according to Maurice M Gilbert who had recently joined from Selfridges. He introduced bold use of colour and brought the styling up to date, but always retained the classical elegance. Ready-to-wear clothes were introduced, and in 1934 ladies' suits appeared. Jaeger first introduced the combination of camel and black and pioneered many other colour combinations, introducing the concept of coordination throughout the wardrobe. They stressed that, rather than 'sell clothes', they 'dressed women'. The need for special dyeing of exclusive colours forced the company to create a manufacturing division which meant that, for the first time, they had control of quality within the company.

JAEGER'S SANITARY

Knitted Woollen Boys' Suits.

FOR ANY AGE BETWEEN 3 AND 14 YEARS.

IN SEVEN SIZES.

THE natural brown or indigo-dyed wool, the excellent and regular knitting, and the closely fitting shape are guarantees for the sanitary perfection of this outer-clothing for boys. The suits are tasteful, cheap, and very durable. The Jacket fastens on either shoulder, and when put on or taken off is easily drawn over the head.

Sole Concessionaries

By 1939 the number of shops had risen to forty-two. The Jaeger look was at its most effective when set on its own stage. In 1935 Jaeger moved from Oxford Street to their present shop in Regent Street. Gordon Selfridge was so concerned that Oxford Street was losing the Jaeger image that he suggested that they rent a space within his store, the first shop within a store.

After the Second World War the company had forty-four shops and 3,547 agents in the UK alone, plus numerous overseas connections. It was not until the 1950s, however, that the major break was made with the concept of animal fibres. Now they had to include the easily washable synthetics, particularly in sportswear and white clothes.

The next landmark was in 1963 with the opening of the first Jaeger shop in Europe, in the Faubourg St Honoré in Paris, and from it came the French wholesale company. Today there are Jaeger shops in the United States and many of the important European cities. The emphasis on quality, styling and colour-coordination continues to give the discerning lady, and man, an exclusive range of clothing, but a very different range from the sleep-suits (with their knitted hats), and the combinations of Dr Jaeger's day.

Laura Mountney was born in Wales in 1925, the daughter of parents who lived in London, but who had gone back to the colliery worker's cottage, on the edge of Merthyr Tydfil, for the birth. Laura did not enjoy schooldays, longing for the holidays which brought a return to Wales, to the wider family and the simple life that centred around housework, family and chapel. She saw that these people loved life intensely; she herself loved Sundays on the Brecon Beacons and going to the chapel, although as the service was in Welsh she could not understand a word! Life here was good.

During the Second World War, Laura moved to Wales as an evacuee, but it was not like the old days, and at fifteen she was ready to move back to London. Although it was a dangerous place to live, she had a purpose, looking after her father who was now ill.

In 1943, Laura joined the WRNS. The same year, she was to meet Bernard Ashley, and later said, 'The minute I set eyes on him I knew this was the man I wanted to spend the rest of my life with.' The son of a grocer,

TOP: *Laura Ashley at the drawing board*
RIGHT: *Station House, at Carno, Wales*

Bernard was a year younger than Laura. He loved excitement and wanted to please his mother by becoming more than a 'shop-keeper'.

Bernard gained a commission in the London Fusiliers and was sent to India; Laura was posted, as a teleprinter, to HMS *Dryad* ANCXF, which was to provide support to Operation Overlord as part of the D-Day landing; a few weeks later she was one of the first WRNS to cross to the Continent, although still not twenty-one years old.

After the war, Bernard and Laura met up again and married in February 1949. Bernard described his new wife as a husband-keeper; he agonized that she had to work, but her work with the National Federation of Women's Institutes was to have an important impact on her life. They held a major display of traditional handicrafts at the Victoria and Albert Museum and she was captivated by the high quality embroidery, patchwork and hand-printed fabrics.

When Laura became pregnant in 1953 she felt sewing would be an ideal way to pass the waiting weeks, for she had been told to rest. When she could not find the fabrics she wanted she decided to try printing some of her own. Neither Laura nor Bernard knew

ABOVE: *Bernard and Laura Ashley with their children, Laura Jane, David, Nick and Emma*
LEFT: *A typical shop front*
FACING PAGE: *Laura Ashley furnishings*

anything about printing but they borrowed books from the library, and with Bernard's engineering knowledge they had constructed their first textile printing screen stencil within a month. All the work had to be carried out in the evenings and at weekends, and as neither were good at drawing, early designs were either polka dots or stripes.

They hung wires round their attic dining room to hang the squares on to dry. The dye was fixed on the cloth by baking it in the oven and a cupboard was turned into a dark room where Bernard could do his developing and printing.

A week after they started production, Bernard sold six linen table mats, each with a two-colour African print, to a handicraft shop in Ludgate Circus – the order was worth £1. With this they bought some cotton and some silk fabric, making this into women's headscarves; already they had decided to use only natural fabrics. Laura would hem the squares, attach the small Ashley labels, pack the goods, invoice the customers and do whatever else was needed.

One morning she caught a bus to John Lewis on Oxford Street and persuaded them to take two dozen scarves on a sale-or-return basis. Soon they ordered another six dozen, which took them all evening to make, Bernard delivering them on his motorcycle the next morning on his way to work. Twenty-four hours later the order was repeated.

In September 1953 Bernard began working full-time to increase production for their hoped-for Christmas rush. Laura Jane was born on 1 October but by the time she and Laura got home the flat had become more like a factory! Between April 1953 and Christmas that year their sales amounted to almost £1,500. In 1954 Laura and Bernard formed the Ashley Mountney Company with a capital of £500.

Soon Laura was pregnant again and when David was born they had two children under the age of two; clearly Laura could no longer help with the business. Bernard was

LEFT: *Stratford-upon-Avon's clothes department*
RIGHT: *Laura did not enjoy posing for formal company advertising*

aprons and oven gloves. Local people now helped with the production whilst Bernard concentrated on sales and the development of machinery.

Fortnum & Mason and Harrods asked them to print 'specials', incorporating their company name, but Bernard

now designing his own furnishing fabrics, sold as Bernard Ashley Fabrics, to hotels and other bodies. The designs were very different to those originally envisaged by Laura; Bernard's were brash, modern abstracts, which were popular on cruise ships. A high profile salesman and astute businessman, he never considered failure. Another early success were linen tea towels printed with Victorian subjects. It was about this time that they moved to live in a small cottage, rented for 30 shillings a week, near Limpsfield on the Kent/Surrey border, and soon Nick, their third child, was born.

House and Garden magazine gave them good publicity and by the end of 1955 they had over 200 accounts and also enquiries from overseas. They opened a showroom in Old Burlington Street in the heart of London's wholesale textile trade, and in 1956 expanded their range to include cotton drill

still saw these as sidelines; he also felt that domestic products should carry a woman's signature and so Laura Ashley's signature became part of the design. Whilst Bernard expected Bernard Ashley designs to take over again as the core business, the fate of the company was sealed.

Still they knew poverty, as the bank as yet had little faith in their venture. They moved to Wales to benefit from development grants thus allowing them to become more economically viable. Bernard now accepted that the business was becoming more feminine and domestic, and that Laura's name had to be prominent. She often felt that they should have a shop to sell their products, but to Bernard this was too much like his home background.

By now the Ashleys were living at Gwalia House, in the small market town of Machynlleth, in mid-Wales. Their home was a stopping-off place for local flannel, Ashley Mountney products, or even local honey! Local people worked for them, which included serving customers, hemming tea towels or looking after the children – nobody seemed to mind, it was a team effort. One of the most popular items was the 'Grandad shirt', made of Welsh flannel, an idea of Laura's popular with students at Aberystwyth University.

Bernard commuted back to Kent for almost two years, until they converted a disused social club at Tygrith into a production unit. Still the banks refused to help, leaving him with a bitterness towards them. However, after two months of moving machinery, they were able to employ some more local staff.

Laura had a maxim, 'Whatever else, a girl can always find a penny for a dress', and soon they employed a dress designer. Four times a year the designer would come from Cornwall to Wales, staying only a week or two at a time. She and Laura would study magazines and commercial patterns and would be inspired to create their own range of garments. One of the most successful was a shirt-dress, another the first Laura Ashley Victorian nightdress.

One day two ladies brought in a magnificent eighteenth-century ball dress, an heirloom, and presented it to Laura to give it a 'good home'. She displayed it for about a year, and then made it some companions, full-length dresses some of which were used by brides, others by those who wanted to be warm on a cold winter's night. Her unusual designs found a niche in the market.

Laura lived according to her beliefs and she created clothes to reflect a purer life, rather than that of the wild sixties. It was in this period that Emma, their youngest child, was born. The children soon learned that

the business came first, but Laura cared deeply about their happiness and also about the family life of her workers. When they opened at Carno she would not have a nightshift.

In 1968 Ashley Shops Ltd was formed so that their products could be the sole attraction. The first shop, trading as Laura Ashley, was at 23 Pelham Street, in London. After some creative advertising on the Underground, it soon became a success. Early demand was for maxi dresses with yards of material in the skirt. They worked closely with the press, often producing clothes to match an editor's idea at short notice – it was good publicity. Laura felt that what she liked others would like too; generally it was so. When they opened a shop in Bath Laura discovered the nearby Museum of Costume, and it became a source of many ideas. When they later opened in Geneva, they

ABOVE: *Laura and Bernard Ashley*

soon attracted both Audrey Hepburn and Sophia Loren, who travelled from Italy to make their purchases. Deals were struck to import into both Australia and Canada, Laura Ashley shops opening in both countries. Gradually the media talked of the 'Laura Ashley look' and to keep this image strong eighteen-year-old Jane Ashley became the official company photographer, a role she held for ten years. Furnishing material, co-ordinated wallpapers and patchwork pieces were also added to the range – after all, patchwork was the inspiration of the business.

The 1970s saw a major factory set up at Wijk in Holland. Although Laura was not really interested in financial affairs, she was good at promoting the image. By 1975 the company had a turnover of £5 million, employed 5,000 people worldwide, had three factories and its own jet. However, their first venture into the United States was not a success, the location of San Francisco not being appropriate.

The company won the Queen's Award for Export in 1977 and David Ashley became involved in the American enterprise. His younger sister, Emma, although still at school, offered her guidance as to what young people would wear, stating that existing styles had too many frills and too much lace. Emma's Collection consisted of baggy clown dungarees in vibrant primary and luminous colours, dots and stripes. They did very well and she gave other ideas.

During the late-1970s, Laura and Bernard became concerned about Britain's taxation policies and their effects on business, particularly through death duties, and they became tax exiles in Brussels.

The 1980s at last saw the take-off of the American venture, moving their base to New York, whilst back in Britain they extended the range of goods to include soaps and perfumes, these being marketed in boxes designed by Nick Ashley. The *Laura Ashley Book of Home Decorating* was published, its first edition running to 60,000 copies. In 1985 the Laura Ashley Foundation was formed, which funded, in the main, second-chance education.

By now many felt that Laura looked exhausted but knew that she was thrilled by news that Jane was to have a baby in August 1985; a month later she would also celebrate her sixtieth birthday. She went to the Cotswolds to see her grandchild but during the visit she had a serious accident and died a few days later. Her funeral took place at Carno Parish Church, the singing led by the Dowlais Male Voice Choir, which only a few weeks earlier had brought tears to her eyes. Laura had a dream of the perfect life; she had also tried hard to help others achieve theirs.

The company was floated two months after her death and at that time was valued at £270 million. Today it has over 500 shops worldwide.

LIBERTY

The son of a draper, Arthur Lasenby Liberty was born in 1843 in Chesham. He was considered a brilliant child and particularly interested in art and literature. As money was tight, he left school early and, out of necessity, took an apprenticeship at a draper's in Baker Street, London. At least he was near the West End and its galleries and public libraries. If he had to be involved in drapery this was the place to be – near Regent Street and the many shops with Royal Warrants. At the time the shawl was the fashion item to have and he managed to get a post at Farmer & Rogers' Great Shawl & Cloak Emporium on Regent Street.

It was 1862, the year of the International Exhibition in Kensington, and Liberty was particularly interested in the Japanese section with its impressive bronze, lacquer and porcelain. When the exhibition closed Farmer & Rogers bought some of the exhibits which then formed the basis of their Oriental Warehouse, and of which two years later Liberty became the manager. After ten years' hard work he was asked to become a partner in the company. He refused, encouraged by customers that he should start his own business, promising that if he did so they would give him their trade.

Arthur Liberty's second marriage in 1875 was to Emma Louise Blackmore from Devon. Her father opened a tailoring business in Brooke Street in the West End of London. Emma's grandfather lent Arthur £1500 and backed a Bill for a further £1000. When Emma's father died in 1881 he left his house to Arthur and his tailoring business to Emma.

The Liberty business started in only half a shop, 21A Regent Street, which Arthur called East India House. Soon the business

TOP: *Arthur Liberty*
RIGHT: *Advertisement for Liberty's beautiful and 'inexpensive' fabrics for furniture and dresses*

was going so well that its rival, his old firm, Farmer & Rogers closed down. As trade in Japanese products reached a peak and prices became unrealistically high, so Liberty started buying from China, Java, Indo-China and Persia. When he discovered that the quality was not nearly as good as the Japanese equivalent, Liberty decided to make his own cloths by machine. His early success came from his work with Thomas Wardle of Leek, producing what was known as 'Art Colours', later known as 'Liberty Colours'. These new silks in 'Liberty Colours' were draped over fretwork screens and became one of the sights of Regent Street.

In 1879 Liberty's showed Umritza Cashmere, a material which had the lightness and softness of the oriental material but also had a greater durability and a closer weave. Many fabrics were still imported from the Far East and he began printing oriental designs, which were reproductions of old Indian prints. The costumes for Gilbert and Sullivan's *Patience* and *The Mikado* were made with Liberty fabrics. In preparation for *The Mikado* he sent envoys to Japan to study the clothes worn there and to bring back exactly the right materials for the cast and stage sets.

As trade expanded, a wholesale section was introduced. The shop consisted of seven departments: Silks, Embroideries, Furniture, Carpets, Porcelain, Curios and Miscellaneous Items. New premises further down Regent Street included an Eastern Bazaar with Japanese and Chinese antiques, Japanese dolls and fans. On the first floor there was an Arab tea room and in the Curios department could be found oriental armour, Chinese carved blackwood furniture, swords, daggers and antique blue and white porcelain.

In 1884 Arthur Liberty decided they would open a Costume department with clothes based on historical influences and children's clothes inspired by the story-books of children's authors such as Kate Greenaway.

TOP: *Elegant dress from Liberty silks catalogue, c. 1896*
LEFT: *Liberty & Co was famous for its stunning window displays*
FACING PAGE, TOP: *Invitation to see Merton Abbey hand-block printers printing the Liberty designs (1949)*
FACING PAGE, BOTTOM: *Liberty's design for Saracen-style drawing-room*

Liberty gowns ensured that the wearer was noticed, so unique were the designs and fabrics.

The name of Liberty's was now spreading far beyond London. In 1887 they opened a shop in Birmingham, and then one in Paris and there were agent representatives in New York, Toronto, Shanghai and Tasmania. The company went public in 1894. Emma Liberty's nephew, Harold Blackmore, through his involvement with the firm of solicitors who sold the company, joined the board of Liberty's in 1900 and thirty years later became its chairman.

The Edwardian era was a prosperous one and Liberty's became involved in decorating hotels and homes of the wealthy, both in England and abroad. In 1913 Arthur received a knighthood and a year later named his nephew, Ivor Stewart, as his heir. Arthur died in May 1917, leaving a fortune of £350,000 but he also had been generous to the church, village and community.

After the war years many changes took place, not least among them the rebuilding of Regent Street to a set formula, the site being Crown land. Liberty's had bought adjoining freehold sites and on this area which formed an island they could do as they wished. Arthur Liberty had always loved Tudor styles of architecture and the new building would combine the best features from that period, coupled with the needs and technology of the twentieth century.

The intimacy of the style gave small rooms in which furniture and related items could be seen in a scale to which the customer could relate. The outer wall gave the appearance of a row of shops, rather than one large store. Detailing incorporated lead drain pipes and handmade roofing tiles while the windows were leaded. High above the entrance was a model of the *Mayflower*, worked in gilded copper, while at the doorway there were the coats of arms of the six wives of Henry VIII, and on the gable facing onto Regent Street were to be found the arms of Queen Elizabeth I. Inside the new building were deep galleries, four storeys high, resembling the courtyards of old English inns. The details of the rooms were unique with their carved balustrades, oak staircases and floors made of deck timbers.

Following the Second World War the new word was 'design' and for the first time the store employed a window display designer. In 1969 when the Sadler's Wells Opera Company revived *Patience* they again used Liberty fabrics for the costumes. Still Liberty's progresses into the future and Arthur Lasenby Liberty would be proud of the store that bears his name!

Lillywhites

In 1835, two years before Victoria was crowned Queen, Sussex lost a game of cricket by three wickets 'in absence of Lillywhite'. Already the Lillywhites had become a great family name in County cricket. The absentee was Frederick William Lillywhite, generally known as William, but also known as 'Non-pareil' because of his round-arm bowling.

His oldest son, James, was born in 1825. He was to become the founder of *Lillywhite's Cricketer's Annual* and also the shop. The second son, John, born the following year became a fine batsman and a member of the all-professional team which went to play matches in Canada and America. Frederick the third son, born in 1829, invented a portable press to print score cards and went with the team as official scorer and press agent. In the Long Room at Lord's there is a photograph of this first of all touring XIs on board ship, wearing the white shirts with pink spots, which were the correct cricketing clothes of the day. Those early cricketing teams had to endure long and dangerous voyages, some braving the unknown terrors of the Pacific.

Fred Lillywhite, the score card printer, went into partnership with John Wisden to run a cricket and cigar depot, but this was dissolved three years later. When Wisden published his *Cricketer's Almanack* in 1864, it created rivalry with John Lillywhite who in 1849 had introduced *Lillywhite's Guide to Cricketers*. Lillywhite's publication continued until 1900, becoming known as *James Lillywhite's Cricketer's Annual*, or as 'The Red Lillywhite' because of the colour of its cover.

John Lillywhite exhibited at the International Exhibition of 1862 and perhaps it was as a result of the interest shown that the shop, James Lillywhite, opened in 1863. It was an interesting period in cricket for the following year's *Lillywhite's Cricketer's Companion* reported a cautious 'Mr W G Grace promises to be a good bat'. In 1877 James Lillywhite, cousin of the founder, financed the first game, later called the first Test Match, against Australia where he captained an all-professional team.

In the Victorian era many sports commenced or grew rapidly, especially among the new middle classes; the emancipation of women also led to them participating in or watching sport. Ladies became involved in archery from 1846; croquet, originating in the south of France, was played in Britain in 1856; badminton began at Badminton House in 1863; while an early athletics meeting was held at Exeter College, Oxford in 1850. In 1890 the Original English Lady Cricketers' Club had been formed. Lillywhites were responsible for equipping and dressing the teams. In the 1890s they wore calf-length dresses with sashes, sailor collars and cricket caps and the batswomen and wicket-keeper wore pads. Lillywhites are still the official suppliers to the All England Women's Cricket Association.

Lillywhites were advertising tennis rackets and lawn tennis balls in 1880, only six years after Major Wingfield had taken out a patent for 'a new and improved court for playing the ancient game of tennis'. In those days the racquets were pear-shaped and the service action was underarm. Similarly in 1878 *James Lillywhite's Cricketer's Annual* had carried an advertisement for an agent handling no fewer than twenty-four different makes of bicycle; later they themselves became agents for bicycles and tricycles.

As hockey, polo and lacrosse became established sports so Lillywhites provided both equipment and clothing for the players. Towards the close of the century skiing was developed as a sport and this was to be very important to the

FACING PAGE, TOP: *Team in Sydney, 1859*
FACING PAGE, BOTTOM & THIS PAGE, RIGHT: *Ski clothes' advertisements, ten years apart*
TOP: *Ladies' golf attire, 1938*

LEFT: *Winter sportswear, 1930–31*
BELOW: *Lillywhites caters for all occasions*

company. Following the events of August 1914, professional sport ceased and international matches were cancelled until the end of hostilities.

In 1922 Lillywhites was acquired by I H Benedictus who was joined as co-director by Major Gretton who was an expert on skiing. The company quickly established itself as the expert on winter sports equipment, this being reinforced when Mr Nat Garrett, later to become managing director of Lillywhites, became junior vice president of the Ski Club of Great Britain. It was Major Gretton who described Lillywhites as the 'University of the Sports Trade'.

In 1925 Lillywhites moved from their premises in the Haymarket to the Criterion Buildings overlooking Piccadilly Circus and their catalogue for that year listed equipment for thirty-four different sports. At the end of the decade, indoor ice skating was the craze.

The 1930s were also important for a dry ski school was created in the Criterion Building, artificial snow being made from chemically treated soda. Their new catalogue showed the 'Lillisport Aviation Suit for Ladies', as designed for Amy Johnson to wear on her first solo flight to Australia.

Throughout the years of the Second World War, the company became deeply involved in the war effort, including fitting out the 900 men of the skiing battalion in Norway. Other special works included making the famous WVS frocks, paratroop boots to a model of a pair taken from a German prisoner, string vests for troops and the supply of 12½ tons of ski wax packed in 4oz tubes!

Today, Lillywhites, Royal Warrant holders to Queen Elizabeth II, still have the reputation of being Britain's most famous sports store, if not the most famous in the world. Not only does Lillywhites overlook Eros but there are Lillywhites at Heathrow Airport and at the famous Pilmour Links Golf Course near Edinburgh.

Lloyds Bank

There were two factors which gave rise to the formation of one of today's leading banks. The first was the concern of merchants that Charles I would seize their monies, which were kept at the Tower Mint for safekeeping; the second was the persecution of Quakers, who in many areas of life developed business interests very successfully, not least due to their frugal lifestyle.

The Bank of England was formed in 1694 to raise money to finance William III's wars against France. Its backers loaned money to the Government and in return they had the privilege of being the only joint stock bank in England. At first many banks issued their own bank notes but later used only those of the Bank of England. Individual banks opened accounts at the Bank of England, made payments to one another by drawing cheques on their accounts, and so gradually the Bank became the banker's bank.

George Fox, the founder of the Society of Friends, often known as the Quakers, preached spiritual truths and peaceful ways. Being a powerful speaker he attracted large numbers to his cause, among these Charles Lloyd. Charles and Elizabeth Lloyd suffered much for their beliefs, being both put into prison and also having their goods distrained, goods worth several pounds being sold to pay a tithe of only a few shillings. Charles Lloyd travelled widely on behalf of the Quakers, finally settling in Birmingham where he died in 1698. Charles and Elizabeth had two sons, Charles and Sampson, who were also hounded for their religious principles. They married daughters of a very

TOP: *Head office, Lombard Street, London*
RIGHT: *Seven-shilling banknote, exclusive to Lloyds Bank*

successful businessman, Ambrose Crowley, who dealt in iron and related products; both sons were to become very involved in such ventures. It was through Sampson's son that the banking link was formed.

In 1765 Taylors & Lloyds opened for business at Dale End in Birmingham. The partners were John Taylor, a prominent button-maker, and Sampson Lloyd II, then an ironmonger, and their two sons, each having put up £2000 capital. Both sons soon joined the London banking partnership of Hanbury, Taylor, Lloyd and Bowman. As well as being an influential button-maker, John Taylor was also High Sheriff of Warwickshire, had bought the Lord of the Manor of Yardley and owned Bordesley Hall. Samuel Lloyd was not as rich but had interests in iron and controlled water rights on the River Trent.

The Birmingham bank was very successful and by 1775 it had 277 customers on its books, most of them traders and small manufacturers. In those early days the bank issued its own bank notes, including an unusual seven-shilling note, which was issued to cope with a problem of a shortage of small change. The bank would purchase stocks for customers, making investments on their own account, including India Bonds and Birmingham Canal Navigation Shares.

Throughout the country dozens of small banks started to do business and of those founded during the last two decades of the eighteenth century no less than forty-two became part of Lloyds in later years. Samuel Lloyd had seven children, who all married Quakers, giving him forty-four grandchildren, who in turn had 120 children between them!

In 1826 the Government allowed the formation of joint stock banks, the aim being to strengthen existing partnerships as in the previous year a great financial crisis had broken out leading to sixty banks failing. Lloyds had anticipated the problem, and had extra money sent up from London and so was able to survive.

Birmingham was now developing into a centre of communication with the railway line from London to Liverpool passing through the town. There were also strong links by water using the canal system.

The last of the Taylors interested in banking died in 1840 and just over a decade later the Lloyds were left as proprietors, but before this the bank moved its headquarters to James Taylor's family premises in the High Street. 1853 saw the formation of a new partnership, Lloyds and Company. However, among the public there was still

concern about the banks' ability to meet the promise to repay. In 1856 several railway stations in the Birmingham area refused to accept payments in the notes of local banks, but again Lloyds had cash in hand and avoided any difficulties. To strengthen their financial base they merged in 1865 with another local bank and became Lloyds Banking Company Limited, with seven offices, a staff of 50 and 4,525 accounts. When the bank became a limited liability company, the issue of shares was very much oversubscribed. A few years later, Sampson Samuel Lloyd became the company chairman.

The London partnership had been formed in 1771, by the sons of the two founding fathers in Birmingham, but almost a century later it had become Messrs Barnett, Hoares and Lloyd. In 1884 the new company merged with Lloyds, bringing with them the sign under which they had traded – the sign of the Black Horse. The sign had been in existence for 300 years, being originally used by Humphrey Stokes, a goldsmith and banker whose name appeared in the oldest printed list of London merchants and bankers, published in 1677, as keeping 'Running Cashes', roughly the equivalent of current accounts.

By 1885, Lloyds had fifty-three offices with almost 34,000 accounts, but by the end of the First World War, after it acquired the Capital and Counties Bank, it had grown to 1,500 offices and almost one million accounts. In 1923 Lloyds acquired the historic Cox & Co, bankers to the Army and Royal Air Force, and also Henry S King, East India agents, who gave Lloyds their first entry to the Indian sub-continent.

The Access Credit Card was created in 1971 as a result of the coming together of Lloyds, Midland and National Westminster Banks, forming the Joint Credit Card Company.

FACING PAGE: *Sampson Lloyd II*
ABOVE LEFT: *Early Black Horse sign*
BELOW: *Advertisement in* Punch*, 1949*

A Matter of Credit

The banking business of Taylors and Lloyds opened in 1765, the year when James Watt first saw the possibilities of his steam engine. But between Watt's dream and its practical expression there were lean years when James Watt and his partner Matthew Boulton suffered discouragement. Their inventions were eyed with suspicion and their slender means dwindled.

It was then that the foresight of Sampson Lloyd the banker came to their aid. He assisted them liberally.

The spirit of the founder still lives in Lloyds Bank today. Many prosperous businesses have been helped to success by its foresight and encouragement.

LLOYDS BANK
LIMITED
HEAD OFFICE: *71, Lombard Street, London, E.C.3*

1677

MAPPIN & WEBB

As far back as 1621 we find Otto Mappen listed among the cutlers in Sheffield. There was also a Joseph Mappen listed as a cutler in 1676, but it was not until 1774 that Jonathan Mappin opened a small silver workshop in the town.

It is difficult to piece together those early days but we do know that Jonathan was the son of Joseph Mappin who was a baker. He was first apprenticed to Henry Bolsover, but when he died Jonathan became apprenticed in 1750 to John Brookes who was a cutler. He is likely to have completed his apprenticeship in about 1753 or 1754. The year after the Sheffield Assay Office commenced in 1773, there is record of him having a mark recorded and in 1775 J Mappin & Co entered their mark at the Sheffield Assay Office. There is still in existence a pair of sugar tongs with their mark and date of 1779. The firm's early address was Fargate near to the centre of the town. During the next forty years they had various addresses and designations which included Plate & Cup Maker, Clasp & Dog Collar maker and Engravers.

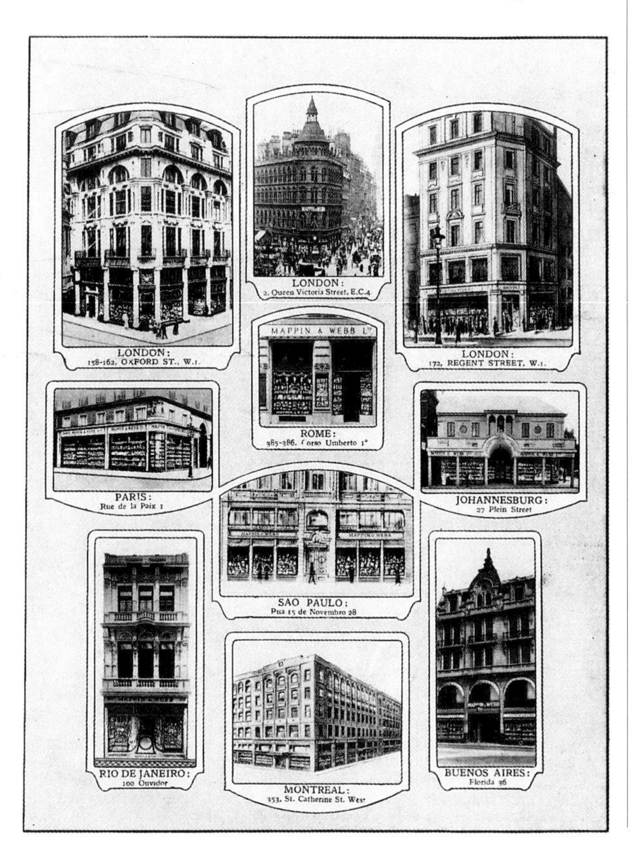

In 1832 Joseph Mappin & Son were listed as engravers, Joseph being a Freeman of the Cutlers Company. He had two sons, the eldest also Joseph, and the younger John Newton Mappin to whom the business passed. John Newton later passed the business to his nephew J Y Cowlishaw who changed the firm to his own name and became well known in the pearl-handled cutlery trade. John having given the business away then founded Mappin's Brewery, dying a rich man and leaving monies for the provision of a civic art gallery, today known as the Mappin Art Gallery.

John Newton's brother, Joseph, set up a spring-knifemaking business in Norfolk Street and Mulberry Street, later specializing in pen, pocket, sporting and table knives as well as razors. He traded as Joseph Mappin, but died in his early forties leaving instructions that the business could not be disposed of until the youngest of his four sons had been in the business four years. The eldest son, Frederick Thorpe Mappin, took up the management of the business after his father's death, and as his brothers came of age he brought them in as active members of the firm. In 1851 the firm became known as Mappin Bros and had moved to bigger premises in Sheffield. By now they had also opened a shop at 17 Fore Street, near London Wall, later moving to a site in Moorgate Street before finally

FACING PAGE: *Mappin & Webb shops around the world, 1912*
RIGHT: *Part of 1953 advertisement*
BELOW: *Page from 1903 catalogue showing a gentleman's dressing and travelling bag*

moving to 67/8 King William Street which was an excellent site and where they became very well known.

At the Great Exhibition at the Crystal Palace in 1851 they, along with people from every part of the British Empire, laid out the finest of their goods. Perhaps it was from this exhibition that the brothers gained the idea of expanding overseas. By 1858 the company was employing 500 skilled plate workers and also had agencies for their products in America, Canada, Australia and other parts of the world. Soon after the youngest, John Newton Mappin, joined the business, there came dissension and Frederick and John left the business, Frederick buying the steel mill of Thos Turton & Sons. He also became a Liberal Member of Parliament and was later given a baronetcy.

It was John Newton who took George Webb, his brother-in-law into partnership. Prior to this partnership John had started a plate and cutlery business known as Mappin & Co, opening his first London shop in Oxford Street in 1860.

A Royal Warrant had been granted to William Samson whose business they acquired in 1845; this was as Purveyor of Cutlery to His Majesty; a further Royal Warrant had been granted to Messrs Gibson & Langman in 1892, a company they acquired in 1903. In 1908 Mappin & Webb became a public company.

Gradually the company grew, as large contracts were won to equip hotels, restaurants, clubs, military messes, and shipping and railway companies throughout the world. After the First World War some of the more expensive lines were phased out and jewellery, watches, clocks and fancy goods were introduced to a much larger extent. To meet the increasing demands of the shops, which by now included Number One, Rue de la Paix in Paris, a new modern factory was built in Queens Road in Sheffield. Other retail operations commenced in places such as Nice, Johannesburg, Biarritz, Monte Carlo, Rome,

São Paulo, Bombay. Royal Warrants have been granted, these dating from Queen Victoria through to our present Queen Elizabeth II, also by foreign royalty and heads of state.

Some of those earlier orders were quite remarkable, such as one from an Indian Maharajah, who ordered a complete set of bedroom furniture in sterling silver.

John Newton Mappin was closely associated with all the activities of the firm until his sudden death in 1913 in the grounds of his home, Headley Park in Surrey.

Succeeding decades have brought new opportunities and difficulties but Mappin & Webb have faced up to each in different

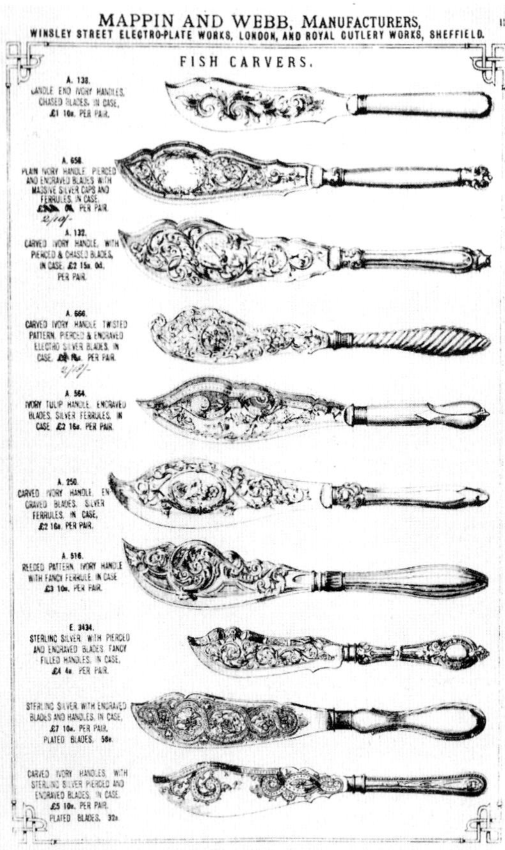

ways. Immediately following the end of the Second World War the company won commissions to equip the new merchant vessels *Canberra* and *Oriana* with cutlery with special new designs.

In the 1960s the company followed an expansionist policy and new shops were opened in several major British cities, while

LEFT: *John Newton Mappin*
ABOVE: *Selection of fish carvers*
FACING PAGE, TOP LEFT: *Mappin & Webb symbol*
FACING PAGE, TOP RIGHT: *Silver bedroom suite made for a maharajah*
FACING PAGE, BOTTOM: *George Webb*

on the Continent branches were opened in Dusseldorf and Cannes. Other links were formed with Japan where a branch was opened in Tokyo's finest department store, Mitsukoshi.

The 1970s saw the store being taken over by the Sears Group who decided that the European developments were not proving profitable and that in future efforts should be concentrated in Britain and Japan.

A further change of ownership was to come about in the 1980s when a deal was created which brought together Asprey and Garrard, both jewellers supplying the upper end of the market, and Mappin & Webb. Naim Attallah, group chief executive of Asprey PLC, was appointed managing director of Mappin & Webb and his new and dynamic ideas brought about a relaunch of the company in 1990. Today its merchandise is more affordable and its stores are more accessible to the public, but still there is a desire to supply the exclusive items of style and quality. Since its relaunch, new shops have opened at, among others, Terminals 3 and 4 at Heathrow Airport, in London's Oxford Street, Guildford, Kingston and even Prague.

Today, fine watches are still produced exclusively for the company in Switzerland, reproduction Georgian carriage clocks combine the best of the old with the technology of the new, while sleek silver fountain pens mix with ultra-modern *objets d'art* and delicate bone china and crystal.

MARKS & SPENCER

The story of Marks & Spencer is the coming together of two very different people, a Jew and a Gentile.

Michael Marks was born in 1859 in what was then Russian Poland, his mother dying in childbirth. As a child he would know the oppression, poverty and hardship suffered by Jews, and as a result came to England, settling in Leeds where he knew there was a large Jewish community.

He knew no trade, had no money, no understanding of English, nor could he read or write, but he understood that there was a firm in Leeds called Barran that was helpful to Jewish refugees. One morning in 1884 Isaac Dewhirst was standing outside his warehouse in Kirkgate when he was confronted by a red-haired youth who kept repeating the name 'Barran's'. With Isaac was his general manager who understood some Yiddish and soon they gathered something of the young lad's background. As a result of this conversation Isaac offered to lend Michael £5, a lot of money in those days. Michael accepted the offer and said he would buy goods to that value from Dewhirst's warehouse and peddle them in the villages around Leeds. Soon Michael had enough money to hire a pitch in Leeds' open market, a table about six by three feet. Dewhirst's cashier formed a high regard for the lad as he kept buying items to sell on his pitch. The cashier's name was Tom Spencer.

Surrounding towns also had markets and Michael soon had two tables on the two market days in Leeds, but he also had stalls at the Castleford and Wakefield markets. Dewhirst supplied him with two girls to work for him when he was at other markets. Later when a covered market opened in Leeds, trading six days a week, Michael took a stall there. On his trestle table he would put a chalk line down the centre, one side selling individually priced goods and the

LEFT: *Michael Marks (left) and Tom Spencer (right)*
FACING PAGE: *Simon Marks*

other half selling goods all of which were just a penny. A big poster above the goods said, 'Don't Ask the Price, It's a Penny'. Later when he moved to a larger permanent stall he put up a sign:

'M. Marks: The Original Penny Bazaar.' During the next two years he opened similar Penny Bazaars in covered market halls in various towns in Yorkshire, Lancashire and even in towns as distant as Cardiff. With everything priced at a penny, mental arithmetic was easy and he never kept any accounts. He searched hard for goods to sell at this price and yet still make a profit on them. He would buy in large quantities to get good margins, cotton reels being one of his first successes.

As the chain of bazaars developed, he arranged central management and buying, but had assistants to look after them while he purchased items to sell, sought new sites or supervised the assistants.

In 1886 Michael Marks married Hannah Cohen at the Belgrave Synagogue. It was the start of a happy marriage; they had five children, all girls except the eldest, Simon, who was born in 1888. As trade developed in Lancashire he decided to set up home in Caroline Street, Wigan – a grim place with pit heads and mine shafts. However, it proved to be a good base from which to expand his business being close to his existing bazaars in Warrington and Birkenhead and future ones in Bolton and Manchester.

As the enterprize grew bigger he sought a partner. Isaac Dewhirst turned Michael down, but suggested that Tom Spencer might be interested. Tom Spencer, born in 1851 originally came from Skipton, Yorkshire. He was a large, burly man, contrasting with the smaller Marks. Tom invested £300, representing half share in the business and on 28 September 1894 the

firm of Marks & Spencer was formed. The partnership lasted nine successful years, thanks mainly to their two clearly defined roles. Michael Marks concentrated on the bazaars, selling quality goods at prices his customers could afford, and Tom dealt with the management of the warehouse and office, the transmission of goods and their simple accounting. That Tom knew Dewhirst's suppliers enabled them to deal direct with manufacturers.

By the end of 1900 they had thirty-six branches, twenty-four in market halls and twelve in shops, most of which were in the north of England but three of the shops were in London. In 1897 the headquarters had moved to a warehouse in Robert Street, Manchester. Two years later they built a warehouse in Derby Street which gave better working conditions for the staff, a key concern of the company. Michael Marks now moved his family to live in Manchester, at that time the hub of international trade and

LEFT: *Original Penny Bazaar*
FACING PAGE: *Torbay store, Devon*

culture; they also became involved in the 30,000-strong Jewish community, some of whom were men of vision and successful businessmen, who nevertheless laid great importance on family values.

In 1903 Marks and Spencer became a limited company, with a share capital of £30,000, shared equally between Marks and Spencer. Tom's retirement at a time of rapid expansion, and his death two years later, came as a great blow.

Michael Marks was a man of enterprize and when in 1904 the Leeds Estate Company opened the Cross Arcade in Boar Lane the take-up of shops was slow. Seeing an opportunity he took eight of them on a short lease and opened them as a Penny Bazaar. On the opening day he said they would not close until they had taken £100 and by closing time they had made £175! The presence of the Penny Bazaar helped considerably in establishing the early success of the arcade, and similarly Marks & Spencer realized that it was in shops that their future lay.

After the death of Thomas Spencer, much work fell on Michael Marks and perhaps it was this that led to his early death at the age of forty-eight. There ensued a fight for control of the business. Thomas Spencer Jnr had worked in the business for several years but had neither the ability nor the desire to take over its management. Simon Marks was too young and inexperienced to take on an effective role. The two board members appointed to look after the Spencer and Marks families' interests, William Chapman and Bernard Steel, respectively, were in constant rivalry. Even so, by 1914, there were 140 stores, mostly shops, and also additional warehouses in Birmingham and London.

The shops remained open until 10pm, or later if business was good; staff were given short breaks during the day. Manageresses had two weeks' holiday each year, assistants one week, but even so the Penny Bazaars offered staff security, good conditions and wages. At Christmas, the girls received a gift and the manageress a bonus.

When Chapman and Steel proposed that the share capital be increased to £100,000, Simon Marks, growing up to be a shrewd businessman, urged the board to dismiss the proposal for fear of jeopardizing family ownership. Simon Marks and Thomas Spencer Jnr joined the board in 1911.

Quickly realizing his comparatively weak position, Simon Marks began buying up any available shares, a slow and expensive process. Gradually power swung in favour of the Marks family but it required legal action to resolve the matter. In 1916 Simon Marks was appointed chairman, although still only twenty-eight years old; the following year Thomas Spencer Jnr died. Another of the directors appointed was Israel Sieff, who had been a schoolfriend of Simon's. In fact, when Simon was called up for military service in 1917, and appointed to Preston as a gunner, Israel Sieff became chairman in his absence. Directors' meetings were held in the Bull and Royal Hotel in Preston to enable Simon Marks to attend. Later he was posted to London and resumed his chairmanship. Simon and Israel later married each other's sisters; both were keen on Zionism and the founding of the state of Israel.

The post-World War One years were formative ones for Marks & Spencer, during which period they bought the freehold of many of their stores. Textiles became an important part of their sales and the company created a new image. In 1924 Simon Marks went to the United States for the first time and brought back many new ideas including the news of new accounting machines, an understanding that each foot of counter must make its proper financial contribution to the business, and a realization that the head office must have weekly stock-checking lists to determine stock requirement.

In 1926 Marks & Spencer became a public company and in 1931 moved their headquarters to Baker Street. Also in the 1920s they started dealing with Corah's in Leicester, who sold their goods under the 'St Margaret' label, their works being named after a nearby church. Marks &

Spencer later decided that it should also have its own brand name, a name that is now known worldwide – St Michael – canonizing Michael Marks and also remembering that the archangel Michael was the guardian angel and patron of Jewish people. St Michael labels have appeared on tens of millions of garments since then. It was in 1924 that the green and gold fascia first appeared. Over many years loyalty and quality control have been key words at Marks & Spencer. Many firms have supplied them for over forty years, but Dewhirst's have supplied an uninterrupted service of over 100 years! Marks & Spencer not only specify the contents of goods but also the processes through which items pass. They have their own testing laboratory and also a merchandise development department.

Today there are over 285 stores in the United Kingdom and Republic of Ireland while a further 300 are spread over the United States, Canada, France, Belgium, Holland, Spain, Hong Kong and Japan. Worldwide Marks & Spencer employ 62,000 staff and have a turnover of £6.5 billion. How many times that first £5 has been multiplied!

The founders of McDonald's Restaurants were two brothers, Richard and Maurice McDonald, more generally known as Dick and Mac, Mac being the elder of the two. In the 1930s they moved from New Hampshire to Hollywood to work in the newly formed movie industry but then moved on to another new innovation of the time, the drive-in restaurant.

In 1937 the two brothers opened a small drive-in near Pasadena, cooking hot-dogs, mixing the shakes and waiting on the customers. Later, in 1940, they opened a much larger drive-in at San Bernardino, a small boom-town, about fifty miles from Los Angeles.

In the restaurant they of course used mixers to make their milk shakes and these Multimixer machines they purchased from a Ray Kroc. Each machine could mix five shakes at a time and Ray found it hard to believe that one customer could need eight of these, and so, out of curiosity, he went along to visit the San Bernardino restaurant. At first he sat in his car and watched as a team of eager youngsters, in attractive crisp white uniforms, prepared the place for opening time. He was even more impressed when he saw the long stream of customers starting to form at the order windows and the speed at which they were served, fully justifying the 'Speedee Service' below the McDonald's Hamburger sign. It wasn't long before he also joined the queue; he tried the hamburgers and the French fries, and he loved it.

Mac and Dick were quite satisfied with the business as it was, but Ray Kroc had a greater vision. On 15 April 1955 Ray Kroc opened his first restaurant in Des Plaines, being the brothers' first franchisee. The site was not far from bustling Chicago and it soon became obvious to Ray just how far the operation could go. Within a year he had hired Fred Turner to head the fledgling operation and it was there, in those very early days, that the famed QSCV (Quality, Service, Cleanliness and Value) motto was

LEFT: *Dick and Mac McDonald*
FACING PAGE: *San Bernardino, California, which opened in 1940*

coined, a creed for everyone in the company to this day. It was the soda fountain company that Ray Kroc had worked for who designed the French fry scoop which ensured a consistent portion for each customer, one used today throughout the industry. By 1958 they could boast 'More than 100 million hamburgers served', and the following year McDonald's 100th restaurant opened.

In 1961 Ray Kroc paid the McDonald brothers $2.7 million for the company. Two years later McDonald's sold their billionth hamburger live on prime-time television, and income that year exceeded a million dollars; they also opened their 500th restaurant and Ronald McDonald was created, a clown-like figure with shoes shaped like the McDonald buns, his belt buckle resembling a hamburger and his nose formed from a McDonald's cup.

As the years rolled by more new initiatives were added, among them being the Drive-thru concept – this originated in 1975 when Larry Ingram installed a window at a McDonald's store in Oklahoma City. The Big Mac, which had been the brainchild of Jim Delligatti, was introduced throughout the system in 1968; Jim was one of Ray Kroc's earliest franchisees. Similarly another franchisee Litton Cochran devised the McDonald's apple pie, as the perfect dish to round off the meal. It was David Wallerstein, a man with a long background in the food industry, who suggested that they introduce the large box of French fries, having done the same exercise with popcorn in cinemas; he reckoned that people who wanted a bigger portion of French fries would feel it was greedy to order two portions but would snap up a single, larger portion; Ray Kroc agreed with his reasoning and the distinctive red boxes were introduced.

Gradually the McDonald's story and influence has spread throughout the world reaching countries such as Japan, Canada, Australia and Holland, as well as several others before the first United Kingdom restaurant opened in 1974 – at last the Golden Arches had come to London! The Woolwich restaurant was the company's 3000th opening. More than 1000 American guests flew in specially for the opening. Nevertheless the UK beginnings were modest in scale, with everyone lending a hand with whatever needed to be done. The manager of that first restaurant at Woolwich was Paul Preston who recalls, 'We started off with a near disaster. A party had been planned for the opening and the mayor and other dignitaries were to attend. We were all under enormous pressure to get everything ready in time. Unfortunately, one of the workmen on the site saw the word "pull" on a lever and did precisely that – inadvertently operating the fire protection system! Clouds of white powder cascaded down and covered everything, which is exactly what it was supposed to do. It took a tremendous effort on everyone's part to clean up the mess in time, but we made it – though we never did see the workman again!' Even some of the supplies were delayed at customs and so they couldn't open until after lunch.

Paul Preston had himself come from the United States but he freely admits he had to take on a steep learning curve as they were surprised by the number of hot drinks they sold compared to other countries. However milk shakes sold well from the very beginning, although the triple-thick concept was new to Britain. In those early days, whilst they could readily sell hamburgers and cheeseburgers, Big Macs were slow to take off.

Finding other sites in the UK proved quite a challenge in itself, for there was a property boom on at the time, but through a contact at the First National Bank of Chicago they learnt that Burton's were anxious to dispose of some of their large portfolio of sites. Burton's Geoffrey Wade offered them twenty sites and McDonald's put in offers for leases on three stores: Woolwich, Seven Sisters and Catford. It was agreed that Geoffrey would be a good man to have on board and so the formulation of the UK company was such that Bob Rhea, an American who was franchisee of McDonald's in the United States, had forty-five per cent of the shares, the Corporation had forty-five per cent, and Geoffrey had ten per cent. Paul Preston had also worked for Bob Rhea in the United States since he was sixteen years old. At this time Europe was not proving at all successful for McDonald's and so entering the UK was a great risk, particularly in financial terms. Bob Rhea worked on the principle of finding the right suppliers,

LEFT: *McDonald's Drive-in, Fresno, California, 1955*
FACING PAGE: *Ray Kroc was impressed by the speed of service at the McDonald brothers' restaurant*

the right sites, and initially replicating the American system. Once these were as good as those in the United States, then they could work to make them even better.

Even getting the bun right was a problem, and finding the right potato was another. But as quality suppliers were found, ones who could offer a consistent product, then deals were made on the strength of a handshake, and so it continues today. For quite some time the Corporation did not let the managers see the profit and loss accounts, afraid that the figures might demoralize them! However, when the Haymarket site opened in London's West End, that operation went straight into profit, the television advertising having made a major difference. Sales were affected positively, although there were still only four restaurants in the UK. At the time McDonald's invested £100,000 of airtime with ITV (modest by today's standards of £30 million plus). Today eighty per cent of their advertising budget is channelled into TV advertising. When the Haymarket restaurant opened, the sales were so high that they logged the highest turnover figures of any of their outlets in the world.

Today Paul Preston, the first manager of the Woolwich restaurant is the President and Chief Executive of McDonald's UK. He believes, 'Take care of people today and they will be back again tomorrow'. McDonald's believes that treating everybody – suppliers, customers, and franchisees and staff – with respect is crucial.

Today there are over 650 restaurants in the United Kingdom, whilst worldwide there are over 18,000 spread over some 90 countries. Even on the Dover-Calais ferry you can buy your Big Mac, or you can buy one on Pushkin Square in the centre of Moscow, in a restaurant that seats 900 people and

has the world's highest volume of sales; when it opened 27,000 Muscovites applied for its 660 jobs!

The Ronald McDonald character now takes on a very important role for it is the key to the Ronald McDonald Houses, a 'home from home' for families who need to stay close to their children while they are receiving hospital treatment. McDonald's believes in being associated with their local communities and supporting local causes. On a national level they also sponsor many events, which have included the Tidy Britain Group environmental activities, including the Britain in Bloom competition, the 1994 World Cup football tournament and Euro '96.

It is difficult to say where you won't find a McDonald's these days, but you will find one even above the Arctic Circle – in Santa Claus Lane, Alaska!

John Menzies

In the early days of bookselling, according to David Wyllie who opened the first bookshop in Aberdeen, booksellers actually published many of the books they sold, having made arrangements with both the author and printer.

John Menzies was born in Edinburgh in 1808, at a time when there were no less than ninety-three booksellers in the city to serve a population of only 130,000, many of whom would be illiterate and very poor. When he left school John became an apprentice to a bookseller called Sutherland, where his duties included sweeping the pavement, cleaning the windows and saying prayers with the family. He worked an eighty-four-hour week with a day off on Sundays and New Year's Day. On completion of his apprenticeship he went to work for a bookseller in Fleet Street in London, at which time he made a great number of lifelong friends. Within the city there were a number of learned societies growing up and in 1825 the first Mechanics Library opened its doors, quickly to become the largest in Britain.

On the death of his father in 1833, John returned north and started a business of his own. After gathering together some books to

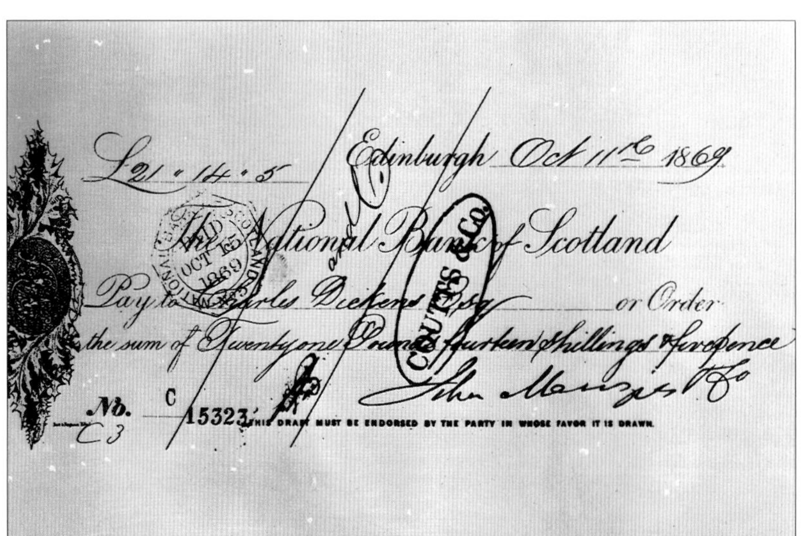
£21 · 14 · 5

Edinburgh Oct 11th 1869

The National Bank of Scotland

Pay to Charles Dickens Esq or Order

the sum of Twentyone Pounds fourteen Shillings & fivepence

John Menzies & Co

No. C 15323 THIS DRAFT MUST BE ENDORSED BY THE PARTY IN WHOSE FAVOR IT IS DRAWN.

C3

ABOVE: *Glasgow Central Station*
LEFT: *Cheque from John Menzies made payable to Charles Dickens*
FACING PAGE: *John Menzies were the Scottish agent for new* Punch *magazine*

sell, he opened a rented shop at 61 Princes Street. Soon John Menzies was to become agent for Messrs Chapman & Hall, who were then handling *The Pickwick Papers*, and they gave him the opportunity to sell all Dickens' work in the east of Scotland. His wholesale business was already taking off. Soon he also became the Scottish agent for the new *Punch* magazine and in quite a short period of time his shop had become the place to find the unusual, the foreign publication, the old or the latest book.

Menzies was innovative in many ways. He started selling the *Scotsman* newspaper, which had previously only been available on subscription from the publisher. He sold inks, pens, magazines, account books and office equipment. He also published four sets of *Vignette Views* and sold 90,000 in four years. In 1845 he issued the first of his monthly Book Lists to retailers (such lists were to continue until the 1940s).

In 1846, the first long-distance train left Edinburgh for London. While the name of Menzies is synonymous with railway bookstalls in Scotland, they were in fact 'invented' by Horace Marshall who had the first one at Fenchurch Street Station, London; his firm later became part of Menzies. Originally they were considered to be centres of vice and places where invalided railwaymen could find work, but this all changed when W H Smith and John Menzies took over concessions and bookstalls became places of repute and dignity.

When John Menzies actually became involved in railway bookstalls is not clear, but it is likely that by February 1857 he had sole rights on all the north-east of Scotland's lines between Perth and Aberdeen, as well as on the first train-ferry in the world, the Granton-Burntisland floating bridge. Another development was the employment of 'basket boys' who had trays strapped to their shoulders and served the passengers on the trains that only stopped briefly at a station. He also put basket boys on the Clyde steamers before establishing bookstalls on them. Gradually his managers were allowed to choose their own stock from the firm's wholesale catalogue, not least carrying a good stock of tourist guides and their famous 'yellowback' novels.

As duties on newspapers were abolished so two new cheap dailies appeared on the stands, the *Daily Mail* and the *Daily Express*. Proprietors needed agents, located in places like Birmingham, Manchester and Edinburgh, who would receive papers in bales, split them up and pass them on to small newsagents, perhaps hundreds of miles away.

LEFT: *John Menzies*
BELOW: *The name of John Menzies was synonymous with railway bookstalls in Scotland*

In 1867 John Menzies decided to form a company and to celebrate its formation a branch was opened in Glasgow. One of the company's relics is a stout leather briefcase with three brass locks and a reversible plate with Edinburgh on one side and Glasgow on the other. There were two such bags and they were put on the 1pm train at either end and were met by a messenger and taken back to the office.

The founder died in 1879 aged seventy-one. He had been a man of his time, having seen the birth of the railway and taken advantage of it. He had seen the early popularity of newspapers and played his part in making it happen. John was succeeded by, firstly, John Ross Menzies and then after his brother's death by Charles Thompson Menzies. Over the years members of the Menzies family have continued their great interest and the present chairman, John Maxwell Menzies, is the great grandson of the founder.

Today John Menzies is a public company registered in Scotland and divided into wholesale and retail divisions. Menzies is one of the two leading UK wholesalers of newspapers, magazines, books, video and audio products, and commercial stationery through seventy distribution depots. The retail division now has over 300 John Menzies outlets, 200 Early Learning Centre shops and the royal stationer, Smythson of Bond Street.

William Murdoch Morrison was born at Chickinley, Wakefield in 1875. On leaving school he worked as an apprentice grocer in Bradford for 2s 6d a week and his 'keep'. Later he worked for a wholesale egg and butter merchant, before starting in the same type of business himself in John Street, Bradford in 1899. A teetotaller, he often had to retrieve his boss from pubs where he would be drinking whisky; this made a big impact on the young lad. William's first wife died in 1919 but he married Hilda Ryder in 1921. Kenneth Duncan Morrison's father was fifty-seven years old when he was born, the youngest and the only boy of six surviving children.

Around the time of the First World War, Wm Morrison (Provisions) Ltd had become an established company; it was now a retail concern, rather than wholesale. In those early days shops within markets were more like market stalls, being enclosed with curtains after closing time, and Wm Morrison Ltd would be among other famous names, all well known to Yorkshire housewives, such as Maypole, Redman's and Driver's. Out of the markets, such businesses had small shops in rows of terrace houses where the owners often lived behind and above the shops. By 1929 Morrison had a mix of such outlets.

Business was hit hard during the 1930s and Morrison had to start again, with stalls in Bradford and Dewsbury markets. His second wife, Hilda, could display the showman's

art of 'pitching' to attract a crowd and she would give the hard sell to people who really had little or no money to buy the goods.

With the Second World War came food rationing and Ken Morrison still remembers counting the little coupons which the grocer had to cut from customers' ration books in exchange for goods. All the family joined in round the kitchen table counting, counting, counting! Bradford's Rawson Market was demolished by bombing, including their main stall, but they had opened a store in nearby James Street; it became Bradford's first self-service store, the prices being marked on the products.

In 1950 Ken joined the Army as a National Serviceman and was posted to Germany. Whilst there, his mother 'phoned to say his father was ill and would not work again'. If Ken wanted the business, his mother said she would keep it until he was demobbed. Ken quickly decided to take it on and was joined by Ken Blundell and Keith Naylor, his brothers-in-law.

When Rawson Market re-opened they took three adjoining shops. They were keen to exploit the idea of self-service shopping, but did not have the money to pay the required covenant for the rent of a larger city-centre shop. About two miles from the city centre Ken Morrison noticed that the disused Victoria Cinema was for sale. They bought it, removed the sloping floor and balcony, and it became their first supermarket – fellow market-traders thought he was barmy, especially to go into the suburbs. But soon his shop was busy with shoppers. The coming of the age of the car changed shopping patterns, and changed in Morrison's favour.

Geoffrey Haggas, who had converted the cinema told Ken

OPENING PAGE: *Modern Morrisons' store*
FACING PAGE, TOP: *Counter service store, 1925*
FACING PAGE, BOTTOM: *Ken Morrison with Jonett Bradford van, like his original one*
RIGHT: *Victoria store, Bradford, 1962*

about some property at Bolton Junction, on the other side of the city, where the owner was going bankrupt. A decision would have to be made that day. Ken Morrison was not sure he was looking for another site, but he went in his van to have a look at it. It was a cold, damp and misty day; there was not even a dog in sight, never mind a potential customer. He believes in having a cup of tea in times of crisis. He went back to his office for a 'cuppa', and bought the site! Not too long afterwards Ken Morrison saw one of Tesco's directors in the store, along with the owner of Woodroyd Laundry, who was showing him the potential for his laundry – Morrisons bought the laundry and it became the nucleus of the Mayo Avenue Supermarket.

In 1967 Morrisons became a public company, Wm Morrison Supermarkets Ltd. Not far from the converted cinema in Girlington in 1971 they built a head office, warehouse and factory complex. The office block was named Hilmore House, in memory and with thankfulness for all the work Hilda Morrison had done in those early years. With the increasing trade in non-food products, the term 'Lifestyle' was coined and registered; the phrase non-food seemed so negative.

Expansion into Lancashire came with the purchase of the Whelan Discount Stores group, giving them bases in such important towns as Preston, Bolton, St Helens and Chorley. Today stores are as far afield as Newcastle and Coventry. Their famous M symbol was designed over thirty years ago and the phrase 'More Reasons to Shop at Morrisons' coined ten years ago.

For a number of years, the company has operated a policy of profit-sharing among its workforce, which now numbers almost 20,000. Conscious of the small beginnings, the company has set up the Wm Morrison Enterprize 5 Trust, a means by which others who want to start in business on their own can receive education and training to help them achieve their goal, being fully sponsored by the company.

Now with about seventy-two stores, their own meat factory and fruit packhouse, they still strive to provide Ken Morrison's original aims from the 1950s, value for money coupled with good service. In 1980 he was awarded the CBE for services to retailing.

It was some time in the 1850s that Moses Moses, a liberal Jew, became a dealer in second-hand clothes in London. A scholar and a lay reader at his synagogue, he however knew the hardships of life for he was brought up in the railway slums of Euston and King's Cross. He had a succession of shops before taking the lease on 20–21 King Street, Covent Garden, and would travel as far away as Edinburgh on buying missions. The other source of much stock was the 'misfits' from Savile Row, and similar quality tailors.

It is not known when Moses Moses became M Moss and it was not until after his death in 1894 that the company became Moss Bros and the business passed over to two of his five sons, George, being given two-fifths and Alfred three-fifths. The other three sons were never forgotten but they did not inherit for a variety of reasons. Jewish families were generally close and would stick together, each caring for the other members and their needs.

It was in 1897 that an incident took place which was to change the whole nature of the firm. Alfred Moss became acquainted with an eccentric stockbroker, Charles Pond, whose luck fell out and he was literally left 'singing for his supper'. Amateur entertainers would frequently provide an evening of ballads and humorous monologues and Charles Pond, while no longer a guest at such house parties, was nevertheless able to entertain. He had long since pawned his dress clothes and had not been able to redeem them, and so he came to Alfred Moss who loaned him a suit for his first appearance. Other engagements followed and he came back to borrow the clothes again and

FACING PAGE, TOP: *Early 1950s catalogue*
FACING PAGE, BOTTOM: *Moses Moses*
RIGHT: *20 and 21 King Street, London*
BELOW: *Premises today, Covent Garden, London*
OVERLEAF: *Saddlery department*

again. Alfred Moss, feeling he was being taken for granted, suggested he pay something for the clothes or even buy the clothes outright which would be cheaper. Pond, however, preferred Moss Bros to look after them between appearances, obviously keeping the clothes clean and well presented. It was from this small beginning that the hire department and Moss Bros's main claim to fame developed.

Over the years, as the company's reputation for being willing to buy up complete wardrobes of deceased men grew, it acquired large stocks of army uniforms, riding and hunting kit and gradually the range of items stocked increased. Gentlemen's fur coats would be beaten with a thin, supple furrier's switch and their top-boots rubbed with a spoon or the bone handle of a toothbrush to take out the natural grease, replacing it with blacking to produce a mirror-like shine.

By 1903, the eight shop assistants would add up the chits, put the takings in a bag and place them in the safe at the end of the day. Alfred would then check these in the morning and enter them on the ledger.

A military department was set up around 1910, and, with the well-established horse-riding equipment department and burgeoning demand for outfits suitable to wear in the new motor car, Moss Bros was becoming the place to find items of clothing for each and every occasion. Alfred Moss was already buying up stocks of khaki cloth made from yarn dyed in Germany.

On 1 April 1914 Moss Bros became a limited liability company. Four months later Britain was at war and the run on military uniforms and equipment was great. Women assistants were taken on for the first time. The lack of female toilets meant lengthy trips to Leicester Square Underground station with a penny from the till, a damnable expense! As with many companies, the years following the war were difficult ones.

Harry Moss, a young director in 1921, specialized in the popular Ready-to-Wear department. As part of quality control, he would try on every jacket himself, having a feel for the correct balance and weight of any size of jacket.

As the years rolled by, more and more influential customers openly came to King Street, and when in 1924 King George V wanted to meet his new Labour Ministers at court, his Private Secretary wrote to the Government's Chief Whip that the appropriate uniform could be obtained from Moss Bros. King George V's death and the coronation of King George VI provided further call for high officials of the court to hire clothes from Moss Bros.

Modern ideas introduced by Harry Moss before he became managing director in 1934 included direct mail advertising and the installation of changing cubicles. In another few years another world war was threatening, and it was again time for change. There was now a need to establish branches, as much to protect their valuable, in some cases irreplaceable stock as to move the firm forward. It was decided to open branches in the main military centres – at Camberley, for Sandhurst cadets, at Manchester, Bristol and Portsmouth.

In 1947 the firm became a public company. During that same year a WAAF officer was getting married and was heard to remark that she would have liked a white wedding but did not have the necessary clothing coupons. Harry Moss heard of this, bought a wedding dress, using the firm's coupon resources, and hired it to the girl, exactly fifty years after Charles Pond had received similar help. The Ladies Hire Department opened and today it still sells (no hiring any more) outfits for Buckingham Palace parties and Ascot days.

In 1946, 400 suits a week passed through the dry-cleaning machine; today thousands of men's suits every week are hired for formal evening and morning functions. Moss Bros has over 100 branches, providing a wide range of clothes for all occasions, with hiring still a large part of the business. In recent years Moss Bros has acquired other businesses including Cecil Gee Ltd and Dormie Hire. Today there are three Mosses in the business and three Gees.

SAINSBURY'S

Between the years 1869–73, John James Sainsbury and his wife, Mary Ann, sold butter, milk and eggs from the little dairy at 173 Drury Lane which was also their home. John had gained a good head for business through having worked for several small retailers, but it is Mary Ann who is credited with 'having the best butter in London'. The counters were marble-topped and the walls tiled, showing that the Sainsburys already had a concern for hygiene. They had six sons, all of whom entered the business, and the family quickly became well respected in the community.

The first branch of Sainbury's opened in 1873 in Kentish Town at 159 Queen's Crescent and shortly afterwards they opened their first depot. John James Sainsbury built up a reputation for his integrity and business acumen and even before the turn of the century the slogan 'Quality Perfect, Prices Lower' had been adopted.

While the early shops were mainly in London the founder quickly saw the

TOP: *John James and Mary Ann Sainsbury*
RIGHT: *Delivery tricycle*

potential of the new middle-class suburbs and established a shop in Croydon. From the 1880s the shops sold a wide range of 'table delicacies', which included cooked meats, bacon and hams, the latter being smoked in their own stoves. By 1900 new branches were long and narrow, again with marble-topped counters stretching the full length of the store, and their distinctive green and cream wall tiles and mosaic floors and mahogany office screens were the basis of a house-style long-remembered by customers. Bentwood chairs were provided for the customer who wanted to discuss the advantages

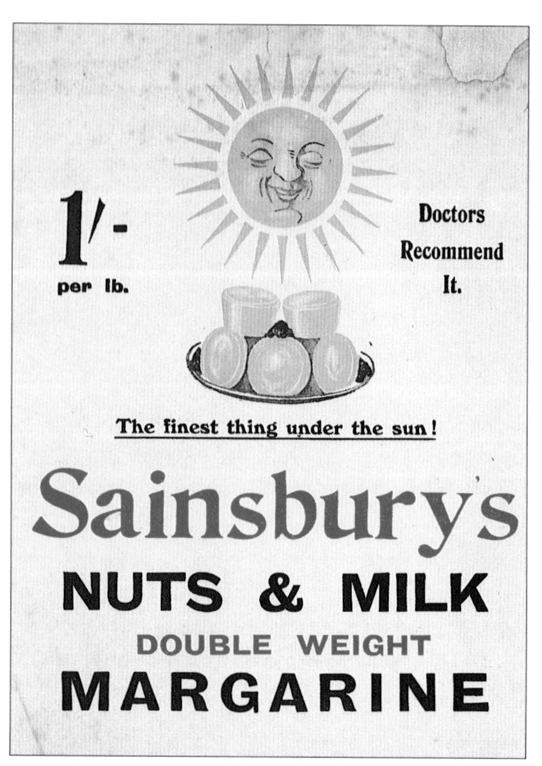

of the various provisions with the skilled salesman, a fleet of delivery lads then dispatching the goods to the customers' homes. As the range of groceries increased so Sainsbury's own brands, such as Selsa and Basket Brand, were introduced.

On John Sainsbury's death in 1928, the *Daily Mail* wrote: 'Mr Sainsbury will always be remembered by retailers and wholesalers' merchants as the man who raised the old-fashioned cheesemonger's shop to the dignity of a profession.' Mary Ann died six months later.

By 1939 Sainsbury's had 250 shops, averaging about 2,200 square feet. They were particularly hit by the Second World War because, not only was there strict rationing of many foods, but also, many goods became almost unobtainable. In addition, their principal operating area, London and its suburbs, suffered badly both from bombing and also from the evacuation policy.

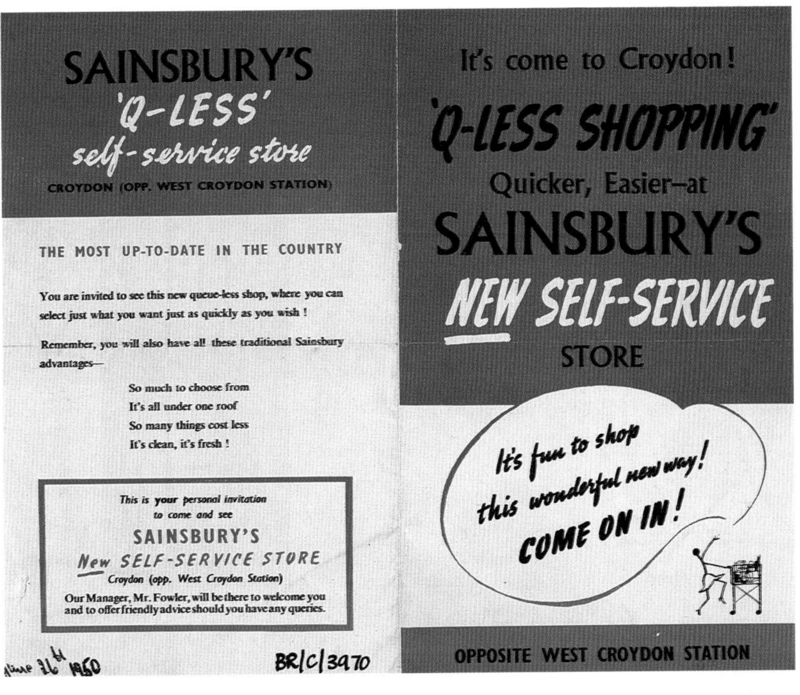

FACING PAGE: *Advertisements from 1913*
RIGHT: *1950 leaflet extolling the virtues of self-service shopping*
BELOW: *Modern store, Woking, Surrey*

1950 saw the introduction of Sainbury's first self-service store in Croydon. The original shop at 173 Drury Lane continued trading until 1958, when Alan Sainsbury, the eldest grandson of the founders, replaced it with a modern supermarket on

LEFT: *Advertisement in the* Daily Express
BELOW: *Leyland delivery lorry, purchased from RAF in 1919*
FACING PAGE ABOVE: *Drury Lane shop,* c. *1919*
FACING PAGE BELOW: *Advertisement for fresh eggs during World War II*

the opposite side of the road. In 1962 Alan Sainsbury was created Baron Sainsbury of Drury Lane, reflecting the company's affection for its humble beginnings.

The 1960s, 70s and 80s saw the range of products offered to customers grow considerably to include household goods, hardware and textiles, and beers, wines and spirits. Sainsbury petrol stations arrived in 1974 at some of the edge-of-town stores. As the 1970s and early-80s had been the times of rapid expansion, both in location and size of stores, so the next few years were to see exciting new developments in in-store technology. The distribution of goods to the stores had already been computerized, and 1985 saw the introduction of scanning checkouts at all the new stores. It was such technology that made the Multibuy, a special discount facility on multiple purchases, possible.

An even wider choice of goods, up to 17,000 in one supermarket, became possible following the opening of the first Homebase House and Garden Centre in 1981. Sainsbury's acquired Shaw's, a chain of seventy-nine supermarkets in New England, USA, in 1987. For all its outlets of Sainsbury's supermarkets, Homebase, Shaw's supermarkets and Savacentres, the group employs over 100,000 staff.

SELFRIDGES

Harry Gordon Selfridge was born on 11 January 1858 in Wisconsin in the United States. His father died shortly after the Civil War and so it was his mother who encouraged Harry to dream. Harry used to sit on his mother's knee and they would play the game 'Supposing'. She had a major influence on his life and career.

His first real job came when he was ten when he started work as a stock boy in a dry-goods store owned by Leonard Field. After a short time working in a local bank, he took the brave move to set out for Chicago. He had with him a letter of introduction from Leonard Field to his cousin Marshall Field, who was a partner in a large store called Field, Leiter and Co, in State Street.

FACING PAGE, TOP: *Selfridges opened on 15 March 1909*
FACING PAGE, BOTTOM: *Harry Gordon Selfridge and his mother, Lois, who had a great influence on his life*
RIGHT: *Selfridges adorned for the King's Jubilee Celebrations, summer 1935*

He was offered a job at the store for less money than he had been offered at a local creamery, but his mother argued that, if he took the post, 'you will be so far ahead in ten years that both of us can have anything we want'. And so it proved to be.

Harry started as a stock boy in the wholesale division but soon his imagination inspired him to seek a move into the retail side of the business. He took holiday time to study the luxurious stores of Philadelphia, Boston and New York and came back brimming with ideas. When he was promoted to retail manager in 1887, he brought many innovations to the store, including new departments for shoes and children's wear, a tea room where mannequins paraded the latest fashions, and, 1882, electric lighting was installed. Every effort was made to encourage the less wealthy customer into the store and window display-tags which had previously read 'Cheap' were altered to read 'Less Expensive'. It was Selfridge who instituted the idea of the annual sale and created the first 'bargain basement'.

In 1888 Harry went abroad for the first time visiting European capitals. He returned to Chicago much impressed by what he had seen and was determined to make their business an international one with stores in New York, Paris and London. Marshall Field did not have the same idea, however, and to keep Harry interested in his company he gave him a very large increase in salary and loaned him $250,000 to enable Harry to become a junior partner. Over the next thirteen years, Harry continued to introduce many new ideas among them the now well-known phrase 'Only — shopping days to Christmas', as well as concepts such as having window displays lit up at night. When senior partnership was denied, Harry left

LEFT: *One of many designs for the Selfridges building*
FACING PAGE, TOP: *Selfridges opens. See the dollar/pound sign on the fanfarer's chest*
FACING PAGE, BOTTOM: *Selfridges' horse-drawn carriage*

the company and bought another store in State Street, but sold it soon after, unhappy about competing with those he had known for so long. After a year of enjoying the good life it was suggested to him that he open a store in London.

So, at the age of fifty, Harry Selfridge found himself in London. Looking for a site for his new store, a Jewish banker recommended the 'dead end' of Oxford Street. The Selfridges monogram was also devised at this stage, the sign being a combination of the pound and dollar signs. Selfridge himself tried in vain to get an underground tunnel under Oxford Street and call the station Selfridges!

The building, with its twenty-seven-foot thick foundation walls, cost £400,000; its opening on 15 March 1909 was impressive. Everybody was welcome and thousands were sent formal invitations, including King Edward VII and the Queen. The store had its own library, a post office, four patriotic rooms for foreign visitors, an American soda fountain, a department for the clergy and a 'Silence Room' where there was a sign which said 'Ladies Will Refrain From Conversation'! Over a million customers visited the store during its opening week.

On 25 July 1909 Louis Bleriot landed his aeroplane near Dover on completion of the first flight between France and England. The next day the aeroplane was on display in Selfridges, where 150,000 people came to view it. Harry Selfridge now claimed that his store was the biggest attraction in London after Buckingham Palace and the Tower of London.

By June 1910 staff numbers had reached 2,000. Impressive window displays and a roof garden enhanced the profile of the company and in 1913 an in-store playgroup was introduced where mothers could leave their children.

Selfridge brought many scientific discoveries to the store, including a seismograph which recorded earthquakes in foreign countries, an X-ray demonstration, an auto-

matic telephone exchange, and an apparatus that demonstrated the first principles of television. In-store exhibitions included the popular penny-in-the-slot-machine which showed the purchaser his photograph in three minutes.

When King George V opened the British Empire Exhibition in 1924, his voice was heard for the first time over crystal wireless sets, the sound then being amplified through loudspeakers. Incredibly, Selfridge had nineteen of these sets available in the store. Selfridge helped sponsor the 1914 Channel Tunnel project and in 1924 spoke in favour of a 'Decimal Metric' system at a business conference, promoting the idea of a ten-penny shilling.

After the First World War Harry Selfridge's outdoor peace decorations amazed London crowds and that Christmas he gave all bus drivers on the route that passed his store a Christmas pudding. He was generous in his private life as well, always entertaining on a lavish scale, and often going overdrawn at the bank! In 1921 Selfridge issued one million ten per cent preferred ordinary £1 shares and received an application for seven million.

During 1922, a young Jewish trousers salesman came to Selfridges, hoping to see and impress the buyer. Selfridge himself passed the young man as he was waiting to be seen, and then noticed he was still there an hour later. Selfridge asked him what he wanted and told the buyer to see him immediately and 'give him an order'. Years later this

LEFT: *Novelties in Sea Dresses*

same man – Charles Clore – would buy Selfridges.

In 1926 moves were made to consolidate Selfridge's financial position within the company and Gordon Selfridge Jnr became managing director of the provincial stores. The next move was to buy Whiteley's, the Universal provider, but due to the generous terms agreed this was to lead to the downfall of Selfridges.

John Logie Baird demonstrated black-and-white images in Selfridges, the first public demonstration of television in 1924. Selfridge said of it: 'This is not a toy, it is a link between all peoples of the world. Great good can come of it.' In 1928 the store opened the world's first television sales department. They even opened a department to sell aeroplanes following the success of Amy Johnson. However, all these ventures cost money, more than was coming in. Following lavish celebrations for the Royal Silver Jubilee in 1935, the Prudential Assurance, who had a financial interest in the store, arranged for Andrew Holmes, a former Midland bank manager, to have a seat on the board.

Things began to take a turn for the worse and in February 1940 it was agreed to sell the provincial stores to John Lewis of Oxford Street. Selfridges was able to attract large sums from the City and the business was put back on its feet. However, the store still had to face the war and, although hit by enemy action, was not destroyed. In 1941 Selfridge Ltd was formed, with Selfridge (Holdings) Ltd, the parent company.

In 1951 Lewis's Investment Trust Ltd bought Selfridges for £3.4 million. Two years later television sets were installed on every floor so that the live proceedings of the coronation of Queen Elizabeth II could be watched by all. It was a record-breaking year for profits.

In 1965 the former young trouser salesman, Charles Clore, was gaining increasing control of the company's shares and eventually won control of the Lewis group. His first venture into stores was the purchase of Richard Shops, and later he built the Hilton Hotel. Clore also formed the British Shoe Corporation which was merged into Sears Holding Ltd. He also acquired Mappin & Webb, and Garrard, the Crown jewellers, and of course the Lewis group.

'Miss Selfridge' was formed in 1966 to provide for the fashion needs of girls aged between sixteen and twenty-one. It later became a concessionaire of Selfridges and Lewis's, but in 1973 a Miss Selfridge department opened in Eatons, the huge shopping complex in Toronto in Canada.

Today Selfridges is still one of London's top stores visited by customers from many lands who know its name and reputation.

Sketchley

Alfred Ernest Hawley, a twenty-four-year-old boy living near the tiny Sketchley Brook at Hinckley in Leicestershire, opened his new business venture in 1885. The idea which he had was to use a variety of vegetable dyes in the processing of wool and cotton shirts and pants. Two years later he was joined by Herbert Clarke.

Alfred had a family background in the wool-dyeing trade and, while the firm was to be called A E Hawley & Co, the premises were known as the Sketchley Dye Works, after the waters of the Sketchley Brook which were so important for the work he was to develop. Alfred had a determination to pioneer new techniques and introduced a process for the dyeing of cotton hose and half hose, which he called Sketchley Fast Black.

Very early on in the life of the new company, great importance was laid to providing social benefits for the workers and others. Such early benefits included the establishing of a contributory works pension scheme, a benevolent fund and in 1908 the Sketchley Dye Works Hospital and Benevolent Fund. Its money came from voluntary contributions from the employees with the company contributing a similar amount of money. It was formed to aid hospitals and voluntary institutions, and to supplement state benefits to needy people. In other cases, it would fund the provision of expert advice and treatment where health problems necessitated calling in a specialist.

While it was a company that specialized in dyeing hosiery, they had already moved into what was to be their specialist area before the turn of the century, that of dry cleaning. As early as 1883 they were advertising that they cleaned curtains, furniture covers, ladies' and children's dresses and gentlemen's clothes. In 1910 they introduced a special oxidized aniline black dyeing process, which had previously only been known in Germany. It was suggested in an advertisement in *Punch* magazine that stockings dyed in 'doubtful' dye turned a greeny-grey shade, and that dye was loosened on warm afternoons which, when mixed with perspiration, irritates and poisons the skin. Their new process was hygienic, stainless and perspiration proof, safe, never-fading, of full-toned richness and permanent.

Alfred Hawley first introduced the French method of cleaning by spirit, later called dry cleaning, into his business in 1889, subsequently including it on his company's letter heading.

The two aspects of the business continued to work well, for in the 1920s as more and more rayon and pure silk stockings were worn so new dyeing techniques evolved and Hawley's Hygienic Dye Works was built at Old Basford, Nottingham. By now Herbert Clarke had become managing director of the firm, but there were not easy days ahead. What with black stockings going out of fashion soon after the company had invested in the expensive development of the German system, followed by the General Strike of 1926 and later the world economic crises of the late-1920s and early-30s, a large bank overdraft had to be incurred to prevent the company going out of business.

In the 1930s they embarked on two separate advertising and promotional ideas. The first was a promotional offer of a similar nature to a GPO postal order – so similar in fact that it had to be withdrawn, although not before it had attracted massive interest – and the second an advertisement for the cleaning of eiderdowns. Letters, carrying a picture of an eider duck, were sent, via Iceland to receive an Icelandic stamp, to homes in England. The letter read:

Dear Madam

This is the eider duck talking to you from Iceland. It is the down from my feathers which provides the warmth in your beautiful eiderdown.
My eiderdown cover is bound to get soiled over a period of time.
I thought you would like to know that Sketchley Dye Works are fully equipped to clean all of me and that during the month of July they are cleaning full-size eiderdown quilts for 2/6d instead of 3/6d.
Please take me along now or arrange for the local branch to have me collected.

Yours sincerely,
The Eider Duck
(Talking to you from Iceland)

By the mid-1930s the company had a network of over 300 branches, mainly in the Midlands and the South East, and its first on-premises dry cleaning site – the Burtol plant. The outbreak of war at the end of the decade, however, saw a completely different service. They rot-proofed thirty-five million sandbags! Hinckley Works was hit by no less than sixty incendiary bombs on one day.

After the Second World War many branches needed refurbishment and promotion of the company came through the introduction of the Sketchley green corporate image. New services were also introduced such as the replacement of zips in garments and the new aid to clothes care, the concept of retexturing. Just prior to the war the company had entered the field of workwear rental, particularly for the engineering industry, but this had now been expanded to cover a whole range of related services.

In 1949 the company went public and changed its name from Hawley to Sketchley and in 1954 the dyeing aspect of the business was removed from fascias, and finally in 1965 the superfluous word, 'Cleaners', was removed from their name.

As we approach a new millennium so Sketchley look to new areas of service with the acquisition of Supasnaps, the photographic processing service company, which now operates in over 350 outlets.

TESCO

The Cohens were one of over a million Jewish families who fled the pogroms in their native Poland, coming to Britain in 1882 to build a new life, free from persecution. Finding a home in the dingy East End of London, and working eighty-four hours a week, it can't have seemed much of an improvement. At least they were safe, and Avroam Cohen was determined to build a new life for himself and his wife, Sime, who had recently given birth to their first son, Morris. Avroam became a journeyman tailor, a traditional profession for Jewish immigrants. By 1889 a second son, Jacob, was born and the family moved to Whitechapel. Theirs was an orthodox household where education was considered of prime importance.

Jacob was a bright lad but had little interest in school. He was forbidden by his father to take a job with his brother-in-law, helping on market stalls; instead he had to join him in his tailoring business, a profession the boy loathed. After his mother died in 1915 he joined the Royal Flying Corps – anything to leave home. He changed his name to the more ordinary Jack in reaction to some anti-semitism, and nearly came to his end during a posting in the Middle East when his lifeboat capsized. On his return to the unit he helped free Jerusalem from the Turks, a particular heart-felt mission.

Mass unemployment and a depressed economy awaited him on his return to Britain in 1919. Relations with his father and step-mother had not improved and he was determined to be self-sufficient. Hiring a barrow, he used his thirty-pound de-mob gratuity to stock it with ex-NAAFI goods and pushed it through the markets of the East End of London. He used part of an existing stand for a nominal rent and soon began to operate in other markets – much to the chagrin of his father who hated street trading. He bought as cheaply as he could and sold at low margins, providing goods that poor people could afford. Not only was he good at selling, but he was also good at buying. He bought a horse and cart to supply his sites in the various markets and found he could do well by also supplying other barrow boys and stallholders.

In 1924 Jack married Sarah 'Cissie' Fox, daughter of a Russian immigrant, a master tailor who made suits for Aquascutum. The same year he met T E Stockwell, a partner in the firm of Torring and Stockwell who were tea importers. He made a deal with Stockwell to buy bulk tea at 9d a pound and

PREVIOUS PAGE: *Jack and Cissie Cohen on their wedding day, January 1924*
LEFT: *By 1939 Tesco had over 100 stores in London and the home counties*
FACING PAGE: *An artist's impression of the first Tesco self-service store*

sell half-pound packets at 6d each. The new packets needed a brand name – which is how they came up with the name TESCO. It was formed from Stockwell's two initials and the first two letters of Cohen's surname. The brand was quickly recognized and, on one day alone, Cohen sold almost 450 lbs of Tesco tea from his barrows.

Another potentially profitable item was soap. He advertised for agents to go out and sell, sell, sell. The orders came in, the soap went out, but the agents and their takings disappeared. He had learnt a hard lesson. But he never stopped looking for a 'good deal'. He decided to take on Albert Carpenter, who had worked as a clerk for a City food merchant, to look after the invoicing and accounting.

Jack opened his first indoor stall in Tooting Arcade and by Christmas was doing a roaring trade in tinned and packaged food. A second covered market stall was opened in Chatham and he then developed a key retail site in Dartford from which goods were auctioned at prices never before seen in the area. Eventually it would lead to the formation of the Pricerite chain of stores. He opened his first two conventional shops in the same year: one in Green Lane, Becontree, the other at Burnt Oak.

It was late in 1931 that Cohen took steps to consolidate his various Cohen enterprises, forming two private companies: J E Cohen and Company Ltd, and Tesco Stores Ltd, each with a small capital of £100. If he was to compete with Sainsbury's, the Co-op and the International, he would have to play the game in the places they were – the developing suburban sites. He stopped auctioning the goods, instead placing pyramids of goods at the front of the open-fronted shops. His motto became 'Pile it high, sell it cheap'. It was a wonderful marketing ploy, and the name on the front of each façade was Tesco. The shops stayed open until the last customer had left.

Within three years of registering the company, the number of shops had grown to over forty. In 1935, the old warehouse and offices in upper Clapton Road were replaced with a purpose-built building, the first Tesco House located in Angel Road, Edmonton.

The company now had a turnover of £40,000 a week, and, over the next four years, new store openings averaged one a month. Deliveries from the depot to the sites were carried initially in converted ambulances, later replaced with old charabancs and finally a ten-strong fleet of Tesco vans and trucks.

But things were to change. Another world war was on its way. But even this time of turmoil had a benefit, allowing Tesco time to consolidate after a period of rapid growth. Privately, Jack bought a nursery at Enfield, his aim being to secure a supply of fresh fruit and vegetables for Tesco during the lean years of war. Two years later he bought a larger nursery at Cheshunt. From these ventures came Goldhanger Fruit Farms, and a pioneering involvement in frozen foods, canning and later production of Tesco own-label jam.

In 1947 a new private company Tesco Stores (Holdings) was incorporated which brought together all of Cohen's various operations. It consisted of 1.2 million 5-shilling shares, of which he held 1,172,910. Three weeks later, 250,000 shares were sold on the stock market at 15 shillings each. He was well on his way to becoming a millionaire.

Jack had always relished power and control and his forceful style caused many tensions. By May 1951, Tesco had thirty-five self-service stores, mainly due to the innovative approach of his son-in-law, Hyman Kreitman. In typical fashion, however, Jack Cohen wanted the credit. Jack bought nineteen discount stores in London from Burnards, and a further seventy stores, many with cafés at the back, from Williamsons. It was not easy to turn the smaller ones into self-service outlets; the rest of the board felt these acquisitions robbed the company of much-needed capital.

By now Tesco had 185 stores, including its first supermarket, and a purpose-built warehouse in Hertfordshire. Jack's second son-in-law, Leslie Porter, joined the board, bringing significant experience from the textile industry, but a few years later Hyman resigned. Great national coverage was obtained by buying Irwin's 212 shops in the north west at the expense of once again depleting the capital fund.

In 1961, a new flagship store opened in Leicester, and it was here that the fight against the retail system which kept goods artificially high was to begin. Jack set

LEFT: *By 1951 Tesco had thirty-five self-service stores*

himself up as the housewife's friend and customers loved it. The Leicester store had a restaurant, car wash and petrol filling station, and was to prove the model for Tesco stores of the future. Across the group, the Home 'n' Wear section, selling good value clothes was proving to be a major success.

By 1958 Richard Tompkins had developed his Green Shield Company. Based on an idea from the United States, customers would receive Green Shield stamps in proportion to the size of their purchase which could be saved and redeemed for other goods. Initially, his target was the corner shop with the suggestion that stamps reinforced customer loyalty. Later the Fine Fare chain introduced Sperry and Hutchinson (S and H) stamps, and in October 1961 Pricerite committed themselves to Green Shield stamps. Fifteen days later, Tesco followed suit, introducing them first at the Small Heath store in Birmingham.

In 1964, the Retail Price Bill was passed by Parliament and gradually retail price maintenance died. By 1966, Tesco's turnover had reached £88 million, derived from 600 stores. Before long the number of stores would increase to 834. However, family discord continued and Hyman Kreitman resigned for the second time – Jack, now Sir John Cohen, was still exerting stern authority. Leslie Porter became company chairman and would prove to be equally as determined as his father-in-law.

As the country went into a period of economic decline, so too did Tesco's fortunes. They were forced to close some 200 stores and the Green Shield stamps were discarded. Tesco needed a new image. Product ranges had to be rationalized and centralized buying and distribution became very important.

Jack Cohen died in 1979; he had been a legend. Today, Tesco is one of Britain's biggest food retailers, with 519 stores across the country, some with a turnover of more than £1 million a week. Tesco now owns the Catteau food stores in France and recently bought a majority shareholding in Hungary's Global stores. Tesco was the first company to introduce Healthy Eating low fat foods with detailed nutritional information on the packaging. It has also changed the very nature of what a food store should be. Bakeries, pharmacies, restaurants, fresh fish counters, clothing departments, large wine departments and an on-site 24-hour petrol filling station now give customers the option of one-stop shopping.

Thomas Cook

Thomas Cook was born on 22 November 1808. His father died when Thomas was very young and, after a short education, he took his first job for John Roby at a market garden in Melbourne, Derbyshire, for a penny a day! John drank a lot of the time so much of the selling fell to Thomas. Later he took an apprenticeship with a wood-turner and cabinet-maker.

The Cooks were a strict Baptist family and Thomas was baptized at the age of seventeen. His life became very bound up with his Baptist missionary work and the promotion of the Temperance movement. In 1829 he travelled 2,692 miles, 2,106 of them on foot.

In 1833, now married, he established his own wood-turning and cabinet-making business. At the same time he started printing and publishing Baptist and Temperance papers. In 1834 John Mason Cook was born.

The turning-point in Thomas's career was in 1841 when he advertised and arranged an eleven-mile rail excursion from Leicester to a Temperance meeting in Loughborough on the newly extended Midland Railway. The trip took place on 5 July 1841, and included in the cost of one shilling was not only the rail fare but also food and entertainment. This was Thomas's entrance into the world of travel, and by 1845 he was managing excursions for a living. His daughter Annie was born

TOP: *Thomas Cook*
RIGHT: *Leicester Temperance Hall, 1853*

LEFT: *Brochure cover, 1884*
BOTTOM: *Advertisement for Great Exhibition, 1851*
FACING PAGE, TOP: *Thomas Cook first visited Egypt in 1869*
FACING PAGE, BOTTOM: *1903 poster*

the same year. During Leicester's Race Week, he took 3,000 children to Derby 'out of the temptation's way'; the remaining 1,500 'little enthusiasts' he took the next day.

Thomas Cook organized a trip to Liverpool, the port from which all the steamers sailed to the New World. Near to the Welsh mountains with their beautiful scenery and historic castles, he was soon organizing the catering and accommodation, although on these early tours these items were not included in the arrangements. He also published his own guide book for this trip.

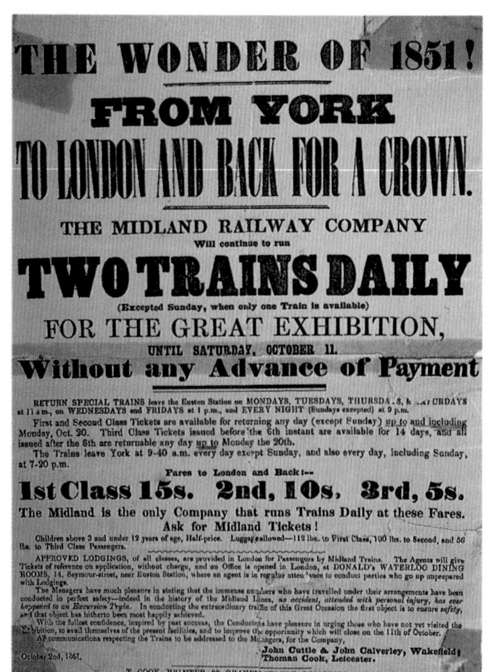

In 1846 Thomas Cook was able to offer a tour to Scotland, which left Leicester for Fleetwood from where the tour groups would travel by steamer to Ardrossan and then by railway from Glasgow to Edinburgh. He had 500 customers, and not enough first-class places for the demand! Railway companies were persuaded to let him issue his own 'Circular Tickets', which were actually return railway journeys but using several railway systems, and they also gave him a reduction in the fare which he could then pass on to his customers. His ticket systems became well known and included destinations such as the newly developing seaside towns.

Thomas Cook made arrangements for 165,000 visitors to attend the Great Exhibition of 1851 which was held in Hyde Park. He provided accommodation for his passengers in houses he had rented, setting up dormitories to provide cheap accommodation for the working-class 'tourists'. As his success grew, so his interest and support for the Temperance movement did not diminish. His comments penned following a visit to Paris in 1863 show how strong his feelings were: 'We never see this great and gay city without mingled emotions of pleasure and pain, especially when we happen to be there on a Sunday ... more than half the shops were open, builders were at work ... the boulevards and fronts of cafés thronged with men smoking and women singing and shouting.'

His tours to Switzerland proved popular among Victorian ladies who found them an acceptable way of travelling on their own. He organized Cook's Cycling Tours arranging for luggage to be sent ahead to their overnight hotels so that members of the group could appear for the evening meal in elegant apparel.

The hotel and innkeepers of Europe welcomed Thomas's extra trade and so he was able to develop the 'hotel coupon', a means by which the traveller could pay for hotel accommodation using a printed note rather than with money which might be stolen. Similarly he used the 'Circular Note' whereby local currency could be obtained against a paper note issued by Thomas Cook: it was the forerunner of today's travellers cheque.

In 1865 Thomas Cook began to move his operation down to London. In 1869 he took his first party to Egypt. Later that year the Suez Canal was opened and this provided a

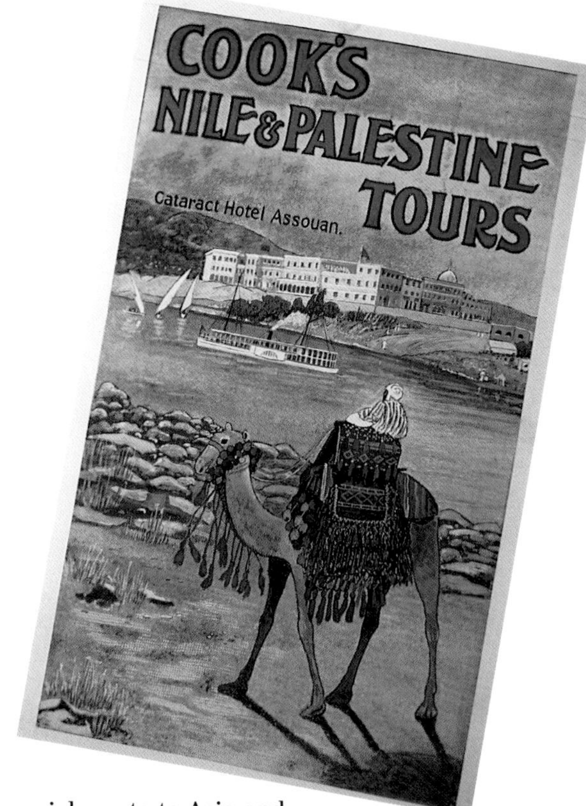

quick route to Asia and possibilities for better round-the-world travel. Cook opened offices in Cairo and Alexandria. His first Round the World tour took place in 1872–3 taking 212 days and costing 200 guineas. The first part of the journey was on a steamship across the Atlantic, followed by rail and stage coach across America to the Pacific coast, from where the party travelled on a paddle steamer to Japan. They then journeyed on to China, Singapore, India, Ceylon and across the Indian Ocean to Aden before coming back via Suez and returning home through Europe. Other world trips, particularly for the independent traveller, included Australasia.

Thomas's son John joined his father in 1865, taking charge of the London office. The following year John organized their first American tour. The firm became known as Thos. Cook & Son in 1871.

A better businessman than his father, John took over as sole managing partner in 1879.

Telecommunication was obviously a big problem in those days so offices were opened in Melbourne, Australia and in Bombay, India. Cook's own newspaper, *The Excursionist*, kept information flowing.

Thomas Cook died in 1892 and his son John died seven years later. John's three sons carried on the business and were quick to introduce coach travel and motor car tours. It remained a family business until 1928 when the business was sold to Cie des Wagons-Lits et des Grands Express Européens of Paris and Brussels.

After the Second World War, the Wagons-Lits Company retained a twenty-five per cent share in Cook's operation, while in Britain the company had become part of the nationalized British Railways in 1948 under the care of the British Transport Holding Company. From 1977–92 Thomas Cook was wholly owned by the Midland Bank Group.

Today Thomas Cook is a leading international travel and financial services group. It has a network of over 1,400 wholly owned and representative locations in around 100 countries. It has three core business lines: leisure travel, foreign exchange and travellers cheques. Thomas Cook owns the world's largest network of foreign exchange bureaux and is the world's largest supplier of travellers cheques outside the United States. It employs over 12,000 staff worldwide, serving some twenty million customers each year.

TOP: *A party of travellers on Thomas Cook's first tour in Switzerland, 1863*
LEFT: *Thomas Cook arranged the first Round the World Trip in 1872–3*

W H SMITH

In 1792 Henry Walton Smith and his wife Anna opened a tiny newsagents in Little Grosvenor Street in Mayfair, London. When Henry died very soon after, his wife carried on the business. When she died, in 1816, the business passed to their two sons, Henry Edward and William Henry. H and W Smith moved their premises to nearby Duke Street, and two years later they opened at 192 Strand, beginning an association that is still commemorated in the name of the company's headquarters – Strand House.

Henry Edward was less interested in the business than his brother and retired in 1828. The business then became known as W H Smith after William Henry, who wanted to provide the fastest and most efficient newspaper delivery service in the country. To begin with he built up the firm as a newspaper distributing house, using a fleet of small carts and fast horses to collect the daily newspapers from Fleet Street and then distribute them to stage coach points. This meant that W H Smith got newspapers to readers at least twelve hours faster than the traditional overnight mail coach delivery. In 1830 the firm chartered a special boat to get the news of the death of King George IV to Dublin twenty-four hours ahead of the King's Messenger.

The firm became known as W H Smith & Son when William Henry's son, also called William Henry, was taken into partnership. It was William Jnr who promoted the first W H Smith railway bookstall at Euston in 1848, seizing its huge business potential. At one stage W H Smith had over 1,000 such bookstalls and some of these became wholesale distribution centres to local newsagents. In 1905 the contracts for the 200 bookstalls on the Great Western and London and North Western Railways ran out and it was decided that, instead

TOP: *Egg-shaped logo and Newsboy with Basket sign*
LEFT: *King's Cross Station, 1910*

of paying the higher rents, they would open up shops on the railway approaches instead. Before 1906, almost unbelievably, 150 of these bookstall towns had a W H Smith bookshop.

Events of later years have proved that this was very far-sighted, for while the shops have gone from strength to strength, the drastic axing of the railway system throughout the country would automatically have led to the closing of many bookstalls. Today there are only seventy-six railway and airport bookstalls, but there are over 400 shops in town and city centres, offering not just newspapers and magazines, but an extremely wide range of merchandise, including books and stationery.

Today the W H Smith retail operation also involves such other well-known high street names as Our Price, Waterstone's, Paperchase and Do It All Ltd, the latter being owned jointly with Boots. Most of the group's retail distribution is now controlled from a modern complex in Swindon, from which books, stationery, toys, games and many other items are distributed throughout the country. The group employs over 30,000 people in Great Britain.

TOP: *Gatwick Airport, 1958*
LEFT: *Kingsway shop, London, 1908*

WOOLWORTHS

Frank Winfield Woolworth was born in 1852 in Jefferson County, New York. He and his younger brother Sum worked on their parents' farm, both dreaming of the day when they would have their own stores.

Frank's first full-time job in a store was with William Harvey Moore at his corner store of Augsbury & Moore in Watertown. At the end of a gruelling, unpaid, trial period, he was offered a permanent job with a salary of $3.50 for a six-day, eighty-four-hour week.

Woolworth's talent for window displays was first recognized when the store launched its '5¢ counter', an idea which was new to that part of America. The aim was to get customers to buy not only the cheaper merchandise on the 5¢ counter but also to persuade them to buy other more expensive items as well.

Even at that time special items were bought in for the sale, and in America such items became known as Yankee Notions. They would often include such things as safety pins, button-hooks, harmonicas, thimbles and napkins. Other surplus stock, items which were difficult to move, were also added and these became known as 'chestnuts' or 'stickers'.

Over the counter, Woolworth nailed a home-made placard, reading 'Any Article on this Counter Costs Five Cents'. Of course he had planned the sale to start on the day there would be crowds in town attending the opening of the Jefferson County Fair. The sale was a great success.

Eventually Woolworth decided to ask William Moore to lend him $315.41-worth of Yankee Notions so that he could open a similar store in Utica, New York. His 'Great 5¢ Store' opened in 1879. It prospered only for a few weeks due to its poor location, although he had made enough to pay back Wililam Moore, buy his wife a fur coat and still have $250!

He travelled to Lancaster, Pennsylvania, home of the thrifty Duich immigrants who appreciated a bargain. He soon found a vacant tumble-down store at 170 North Street and he opened the world's first five- and ten-cent store on the day the

TOP: *Store showing 5- and 10-cent merchandise*
RIGHT: *Frank Winfield Woolworth*
OVERLEAF: *The very distinctive gold lettering on a red background was the Woolworth stores' trademark in America until 1969*

circus came to town! By the end of the day thirty per cent of his stock had been sold. One new line that he introduced was Christmas tree ornaments, which he popularized in America and which brought in millions over the following years. His bestselling lines were tinware, toys, towels, ribbons and handkerchiefs; expenses were kept to a minimum by wrapping goods in newspaper.

Originally, the stores were operated by partner-managers, who shared the profits, but this practice was discontinued in 1888, all the new stores belonging solely to Woolworth. However, even under the new regime all benefited for they were good years in the American economy. To ensure the lowest possible price Woolworth would buy in enormous quantities. His philosophy was to make a small profit on many low-priced items rather than striving for great profits on a small number of high-priced goods.

In 1888 Woolworth became bedridden with typhoid for a few months, from where he learned the important lesson of delegation. He could now concentrate on his expansion plans and selecting good managers, or 'good generals' as he called them. He urged his staff to use thin paper to save on postage costs and insisted that customers should always be treated with courtesy and efficiency. Wages were not high but he did pioneer paid holidays and the giving of Christmas bonuses.

In 1905 the company was incorporated as F W Woolworth & Co with 120 stores. Woolworth's dream to have a chain of stores in England came true when, in 1909, he opened his first 3*d.* and 6*d.* stores. Eventually the number of stores in the United Kingdom alone would reach 1000!

By the end of 1912 the chain numbered 596 stores and the company was renamed F W Woolworth Co. It was a multimillion-dollar business and Frank Woolworth held over fifty per cent of the stock.

Frank Woolworth had long dreamed of erecting an imposing building that would bear his name. The sixty-storey building was designed in a U shape and every detail throughout the building gave a cathedral-like atmosphere. His own office was a replica of the Empire Room of Napoleon Bonaparte's palace in Compiegne! At its opening in 1913, President Woodrow Wyatt pressed a button in the White House which lit up the 80,000 bulbs. Frank Woolworth's dream had come true.

Frank Woolworth died in 1919 and his obituary in the New York *Sun* read: 'He won a fortune, not showing how little could be sold for much, but how much could be sold for little.'

It was not until 1935 that the company's arbitrary price limit of 5¢ and 10¢ was discontinued in all Woolworth's stores. The introduction of self-service stores was to follow in later years and throughout succeeding generations the stores have also moved into the new shopping centres. At its centenary year its sales soared to above the $6 billion mark. Today the company has stores in the United States, Canada, Germany, Mexico, Australia, Spain and the Caribbean Islands. The stores in the United Kingdom are now owned by the Kingfisher Group.

Yorkshire Bank

Colonel Edward Akroyd of Halifax, the founder of the West Riding Penny Savings Bank, described the working men of the West Riding as 'naturally shrewd, provident, industrious and imbued with a noble spirit of independence'. The bank commenced its operation on 1 May 1859 in Leeds, but it was three years before that that a meeting had been held in the Philosophical Hall, to which magistrates, clergy and gentry of the West Riding had come. Originally it had been intended also to form a Working Man's Provident Society, but it was soon decided to concentrate solely on the Savings Bank.

It has been recorded that Colonel Akroyd had been influenced greatly by the Revd Charles Kingsley, then one of Her Majesty's chaplains, whom he heard preach at Whitehall Chapel in London. In a sermon Kingsley had referred to the book, *East and West,* by Countess Spencer about the gulf that divided the rich from the poor and class from class in London. Akroyd wanted to find a way to bring the high and low in society closer together, to help the poor help themselves in provincial towns and in the adjoining country areas. He felt this should be easier to accomplish in Yorkshire, particularly in country areas where people are personally acquainted with each other, rather than in London where perhaps people do not even know their next-door neighbour. 'To help the poor help themselves' was therefore to be a cardinal principle of the Yorkshire Penny Bank.

The Yorkshire Penny Bank's first office was in the secretary's house in Skinner Lane but it was quickly felt necessary to have a central office and so a lease was taken on No 2 East Parade.The bank was registered under the Friendly Societies Acts and its rules dictated that no deposit was to exceed

TOP: *Colonel Edward Akroyd*
RIGHT: *Market Place, Dewsbury, Yorkshire*

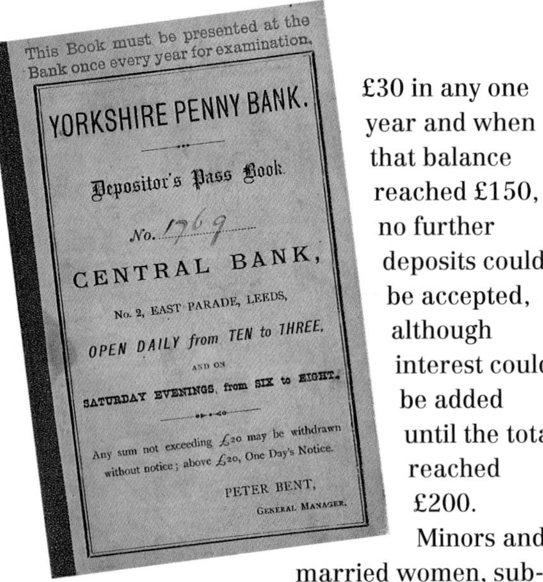
This Book must be presented at the Bank once every year for examination.

YORKSHIRE PENNY BANK.

Depositor's Pass Book.

No. 1769

CENTRAL BANK,

No. 2, EAST PARADE, LEEDS,

OPEN DAILY from TEN to THREE,

AND ON

SATURDAY EVENINGS, from SIX to EIGHT.

Any sum not exceeding £20 may be withdrawn without notice; above £20, One Day's Notice.

PETER BENT,
GENERAL MANAGER.

£30 in any one year and when that balance reached £150, no further deposits could be accepted, although interest could be added until the total reached £200.

Minors and married women, subject to certain conditions, were also able to have accounts. A week's notice was required for withdrawals of up to £5, two weeks' notice for larger amounts. There were also regulations as to where a branch could be located, which excluded public houses and beer shops. Another rule provided that the bank would be managed by a central committee which would consist of a president, two or more vice-presidents and fifteen guarantee managers, who each nominated five trustees from among their number, each having to be a guarantor for at least £100.

Even still Colonel Akroyd perhaps had some misgivings, for he wrote: 'May God prosper the proposed undertakings, and make it prove an instrument to unite in the bond of good fellowship the various classes of society, and especially to promote the comfort and independence, the well-being and the self-respect of the working men of the West Riding.'

The names of those who held office on the central committee was such that the bank quickly acquired confidence, and just as importantly their deposits. At the branch level, there was a similar structure with usually the squire, a clergyman or a schoolmaster as its president. During the first month that the bank was in operation, only two branches were opened, neither in places likely to see such an event today – in Dewsbury and Oxenhope, near Keighley. By the end of May 1859 Dewsbury had taken 105 deposits worth a total of £10.16.8*d* and Oxenhope thirty-eight deposits worth a total of £10.10.7*d*. By the end of that year, twenty-four branches had opened, and by the

TOP: *Yorkshire Bank paying-in book from 1886*
LEFT AND FACING PAGE: *Ink blotters advertising the bank's services*

end of the following year, there were 128. Until 1865, the branches usually conducted business on only one evening a week when they were open for one or two hours.

Sub-branches were set up in many villages, being the only means of saving. They usually met in schoolrooms and church halls. The Haworth branch, with its president Revd Patrick Brontë, however, met at the Brontë Museum, the Lees & Cross Roads branch met at the Wesleyan School, and the Slaidburn branch, to the heart-searching of many, broke the prohibitive rule and was located in the Hark-to-Bounty Inn.

The first bank book to be issued to depositors showed the name 'West Riding of Yorkshire Penny Savings Bank', and was a folded card measuring eight by five inches for which the depositor was charged one penny on opening his account. Later a smaller, more convenient-sized book was produced and on its cover the names of the branch officials would be written in by hand.

The person who received and repaid money was called the actuary, and he had to pass the surplus cash from his branch to the nearest district treasurer. As transport was often very limited and in winter villages could be cut off for a number of days by snowdrifts, the actuary might have to guard the bank's monies in his own home until he could remit the money. Sometimes actuaries would send half notes by post to the central office and when these had been acknowledged, then send on the other half. Not all actuaries were experienced bookkeepers and this led to problems at balance time; in some cases disagreements in the village might lead to the usual venue suddenly becoming unavailable for banking purposes. In 1887, the actuary at Ecclesfield took the unusual decision to provide a tea and entertainment for his almost 200 depositors to celebrate the first anniversary of the opening of that evening branch. Revd Dr Gatty was in the chair and 'exhorted his hearers to the practice of thrift as a duty to the Almighty'. After the speeches, a magic lantern show illustrated the history of Dick Whittington, although it is not sure how this related to the event!

At the outset, the bank was intended to be philanthropic and non-profit making, but even so it was possible to transfer working surpluses to a reserve fund and within four years of opening it was in profit, this amounting to £226.18.9d.

In 1860, it was decided to extend the operations to include the whole of Yorkshire and its name became 'The Yorkshire Penny Savings Bank'. Cheque books were introduced in 1872, particularly for the benefit of small tradesmen, although some felt such a move was making it too much like a

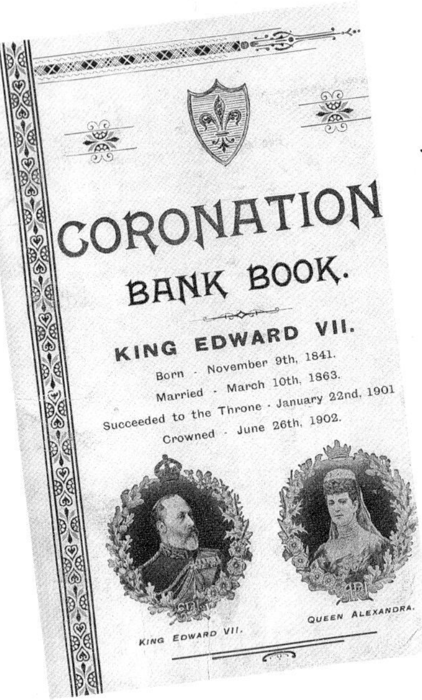

LEFT: *Yorkshire Bank paying-in book from Edward VII's coronation year, 1902*

'commercial' bank!

In 1873 Sir Henry Ripley chaired a meeting in Bradford where he referred to the success of school banks in the town of Ghent, expressing a hope that a similar system might be created in Yorkshire. The following year the central committee opened such banks in primary schools in the county. Although at first far from successful, in 1891 the Free Education Act was passed which brought about the opening of a large number of new schools. Prior to the introduction of the act the bank printed and circulated to parents of school children a leaflet suggesting that parents who had previously been paying pence for their children's education should in future deposit the money in to the Yorkshire Penny Bank School Transfer Banks, to accumulate for the benefit of their children in later life. The Yorkshire Penny Bank was the first to take such action, although others followed later. In all, 150,000 leaflets were circulated, and within three months 150 new branches were opened. In the 1897 report, it showed that 1,902,856 school transactions only yielded £15,256. 15*s.* 0d, and whilst in 1908 the number of transactions had grown to 2,907,427, these still only yielded a deposit of £89,056. 2*s.*5*d.* It represented an average deposit of 7⅓*d.* per transaction! In one elementary school in a poor district of a large town on one day there were 559 deposits made which amounted to a total of £14. 9*s.* 4*d.* and of these deposits 101 of them were of one penny only.

With depositors' balances in the region of £18 million and with reserves of only £½ million, it was realized that the bank needed more guarantees than that of the persons who controlled it. The Bank of England arranged for a reconstitution of the bank, and was taken over by a consortium of eleven banks. It now became 'The Yorkshire Penny Bank Ltd'.

Following these changes, the bank, for the first time, allowed overdrafts, the first advance on overdraft being £5000 to the Associated Society of Locomotive Engineers and Firemen.

Although a girl had had the temerity to apply for a job in the bank in 1894, such an appointment was inconceivable at the time; it was only the outbreak of the First World War leading to a shortage of male workers which led to advertisements for women. In 1918 in Sheffield the Bank Officers' Guild was formed; today it is the Banking, Insurance and Building Union.

During the 1920s self-recording home safes became very popular and within three years a quarter of a million were in use.

After the Second World War, the nature of the bank was to start to change as a full commercial service was promoted.

1959, the bank's centenary year, was also the time for a name change – at last the 'Penny' was dropped and the bank became 'The Yorkshire Bank'. In 1990, the National Australia Bank became the Yorkshire Bank's new owners, having paid £1 billion for the entire share capital. Indeed big oak trees grow from small acorns!